Balanced Trade

Balanced Trade

Ending the Unbearable Costs of America's Trade Deficits

Jesse T. Richman, Howard B. Richman,
and Raymond L. Richman

LEXINGTON BOOKS
Lanham • Boulder • New York • Toronto • Plymouth, UK

Published by Lexington Books
A wholly owned subsidiary of Rowman & Littlefield
4501 Forbes Boulevard, Suite 200, Lanham, Maryland 20706
www.rowman.com

10 Thornbury Road, Plymouth PL6 7PP, United Kingdom

British Library Cataloguing in Publication Information Available

Library of Congress Cataloging-in-Publication Data

Richman, Jesse T.
Balanced trade : ending the unbearable costs of America's trade deficits / Jesse Richman, Howard Richman, and Raymond Richman.
pages cm
Includes bibliographical references and index.
ISBN 978-0-7391-8880-4 (cloth : alk. paper) — ISBN 978-0-7391-8881-1 (electronic)
1. Balance of trade—United States. 2. United States—Commerce. 3. United States—Economic policy. I. Richman, Howard B. II. Richman, Raymond L. (Raymond Leonard), 1918- III. Title.
HF3031.R533 2014
382'.170973—dc23

2014003585

™ The paper used in this publication meets the minimum requirements of American National Standard for Information Sciences—Permanence of Paper for Printed Library Materials, ANSI/NISO Z39.48-1992.

Printed in the United States of America

As three generations who have greatly enjoyed working together on this project, we dedicate it to the future generations of our family, our nation, and the world. May they learn from our generations' mistakes, overcome our deficits, and never stop trying to fix things.

Contents

Acknowledgments

The creation of any book benefits from the assistance of many others. We greatly appreciate the helpful comments we received on our ideas at various stages of development from Ralph Gomory, Giuseppe Ammendola, Alan Tonelson, our students, our colleagues, anonymous reviewers, and readers of our blog at Idealtaxes.com. We are also grateful for our editor Joseph Parry of Lexington Books for his support and encouragement. Any remaining errors are our own.

This work would not be possible without the work of the economists upon whose shoulders we are standing including Giuseppe Ammendola, Otto Davis, Ian Fletcher, Milton Friedman, Ralph Gomory, John Maynard Keynes, Peter Morici, Peter Navarro, Clyde Prestowitz, and Paul Samuelson.

Finally, this book would not have been possible without the support of our family. We are particularly grateful to Wilma, Susan, and Patricia for putting up with our many late night phone calls, the hours spent writing, and the absentmindedness that the intellectual life can sometimes encourage.

Introduction

This book exists because we believe the trade policies being pursued by the United States are guided by idealized models that do not match the real world in important ways. We challenge the often accepted theory that free trade is always beneficial to both trading partners. We propose the alternative theory that free trade is typically beneficial to both only if it is balanced.

The central focus of this book is balanced trade, a condition assumed in most models, but rarely present in the real world. We argue that massive trade deficits have harmed the U.S. economy, and we show how to bring trade back toward balance.

In the course of its history the United States has pursued a mix of three approaches to trade policy: (1) protectionism, (2) free trade, and (3) reciprocal or balanced trade. Protectionism worked when the U.S. economy was small and rivals were less inclined to retaliate. In recent decades free trade has failed the U.S. economy due to mercantilist trading partners and massive trade deficits. It is time for the United States to revise its trade policies in order to end the trade deficits. The solution is a policy of reciprocal or balanced trade.

From the 1860s until the 1930s the United States pursued trade policies built around protectionism and the pursuit of mercantile advantage. Like China today, the United States often offered little protection for the intellectual property of the world's leading economic powers. The U.S. Congress, allied to domestic manufacturing interests that held sway within the Republican Party, erected tariff barriers that helped encourage the growth of U.S. domestic industry at the expense of foreign competitors.

By the 1930s these protectionist and mercantilist policies were no longer working well. The final blow came with the enactment of the Smoot-Hawley tariff and Roosevelt's manipulation of the dollar's exchange rate (in terms of gold), even in the face of the Great Depression and global retaliation. With the British no longer willing to provide unilateral free trade, U.S. manufacturers suffered substantial losses.

Democrats had never been as supportive of high tariffs as Republicans. When the Great Depression swept Franklin Roosevelt into power, Democrats engineered a dramatic departure from historic U.S. trade policy. The key innovation was the concept of reciprocity, and the explicit goal became, over time, the creation of a world in which barriers to trade would be eliminated, a world in which the advantages of free trade embedded in the concept of comparative advantage would produce rising global welfare. Institutions were created after World War II that sought to bring this world about. Unfortunately in the construction of these institutions, the principle of balanced trade, which John Maynard Keynes sought to place at their heart, was largely ignored by U.S. negotiators.

The U.S. commitment to reciprocal reductions in tariff barriers became, over time, a U.S. willingness to tolerate dramatically imbalanced trade. In the 1930s Democrats shifted authority over the tariff from Congress to the president. Since then, presidents have pursued trade policy as an instrument of foreign policy, sometimes in ways that substantially weakened the United States economically in exchange for other benefits. Trade reciprocity—balanced flows of trade—got lost in the pursuit of "free trade." The key failure was an excessively narrow focus on tariffs as the gauge of reciprocity.

Japan, China, and a variety of other U.S. competitors found ways to exploit U.S. free trade ideology. By pursuing policies such as currency manipulation, export subsidies, and non-tariff barriers, they created effective barriers to trade without depending principally on tariffs. Trade was brought and kept out of balance, and U.S. manufacturing prominence across many industries was destroyed.

To respond effectively, the United States must return to the principal of reciprocity—the valid nugget at the heart of the efforts Roosevelt made to change U.S. trade policy in the 1930s. But reciprocity must be defined appropriately. It must require a rough equality of trade flows, and its achievement should include a focus on the totality of trade barriers including the non-tariff barriers and the currency manipulations.

It is impossible to individually counteract all of the many varied and hidden barriers to trade balance. To protect the principle of reciprocal balanced trade, the United States must be willing to enact policies, such as the Scaled Tariff of chapter 9, which respond effectively and automatically to trade imbalances whatever their cause. Only then can the United States ensure that its trading partners engage in reciprocal exchange of goods and services.

We develop this argument in detail through the following chapters. In part I, we discuss the causes and problems of trade deficits:

- Chapter 1 discusses trade deficits caused by foreign mercantilism.
- Chapter 2 discusses trade deficits caused by private savings flows.
- Chapter 3 discusses the damage done by trade deficits whatever the cause.

In part II, we discuss the reasons why little action has been taken in the United States to address the problem of trade imbalances:

- Chapter 4 examines the failure of economists.
- Chapter 5 examines the failure of the U.S. political system.
- Chapter 6 examines the failure of the Federal Reserve.

In part III, we discuss the solution:

- Chapter 7 develops the general principle of trade reciprocity upon which any solution must be based.
- Chapter 8 analyzes the degree to which a variety of previously proposed solutions would efficiently and effectively generate a reciprocal balance of trade.
- Chapter 9 develops the Scaled Tariff proposal which insures reciprocity.
- Chapter 10 lays out the implications of our analysis for macroeconomic policy.

I

THE PROBLEMS

1

The Problem of Mercantilism

The key problem is mercantilism—the ancient and continuing efforts of countries to twist mutually beneficial international trade to a one-sided advantage. The fundamental answer we seek in these pages is how a principled country—which believes in the benefits of mutually beneficial trade—ought to respond to the predations of mercantilist trading partners.

The United States has run a trade deficit in goods and services for more than three decades, generating important policy debates on whether and to what extent balancing trade should be a priority. Classical economists believed that free market forces would correct trade imbalances "automatically." However, the evidence is clear that market forces have been largely ineffective as the U.S. trade deficit has grown higher over the last two decades.

Some economists attribute the enduring U.S. trade deficit to a new form of mercantilism carried out by America's trading partners, dubbed "monetary mercantilism" by Aizenman and Lee (2008), who defined it as "hoarding international reserves in order to improve competitiveness." Under both systems of mercantilism countries encourage exports and discourage imports in order to run trade surpluses. Under the classical form of mercantilism, they do so by accumulating foreign gold. Under the new form, they do so by accumulating international reserves and other foreign assets.

Since 1995, the International Monetary Fund (IMF) has been collecting self-reports from central banks regarding how much they were accumulating in foreign reserves. Although these reports are voluntary and incomplete, they give some indication of the total amount of dollars that foreign central banks have accrued each year, arguably as part of their mercantilist strategies. The dotted line, labeled "Reserve Accumulations" in figure 1.1, shows our estimate of the amount of new dollars added to reserves by foreign governments each year since 1996, the first year during which the growth in reserves from one year to the next could be calculated.

Figure 1.1. Mercantilism and the U.S. Trade Deficit

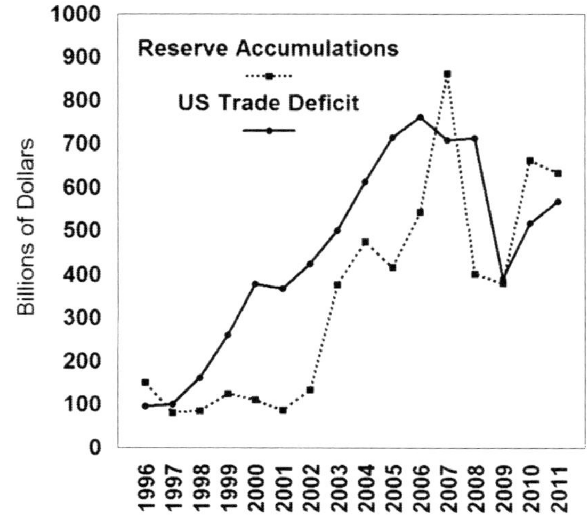

Reserve accumulations are the annual change in foreign government dollar reserves from the IMF's COFER database, estimating that the proportion of dollars in unallocated reserves is the same as the proportion in allocated reserves. Source for the U.S. trade deficit (goods and services) is the BEA.

As shown by the figure, since about 2003, foreign central bank accumulations of dollars have been large enough to finance just about the entire U.S. trade deficit. These reserve accumulations have prevented foreign currencies from rising and the U.S. dollar from falling to trade-balancing exchange rates.

Japan first employed mercantilism in the years following World War II. They targeted the market shares of one American industry after another for takeover by their producers. Then Taiwan, the Asian Tigers, and China copied the policy that had converted Japan from a weak and backward economy to a world powerhouse. In recent years, more and more countries have been joining the bandwagon, with the United States as their primary target. They have accumulated U.S. assets in order to manipulate currency exchange rates and to preserve the conditions that produce trade surpluses for them and trade deficits for the United States. China's foreign exchange reserves are now larger than those of all of the other countries of the world combined. Navarro and Autry (2011, 2) summarized the disastrous effect of Chinese mercantilism upon the U.S. economy:

> China's "weapons of job destruction" include massive illegal export subsidies, the rampant counterfeiting of U.S. intellectual property, pitifully lax environmental protections, and the pervasive use of slave labor. The centerpiece of Chinese mercantilism is,

> however, a shamelessly manipulated currency that heavily taxes U.S. manufacturers, extravagantly stimulates Chinese exports, and has led to a ticking time bomb U.S.–China trade deficit close to a *billion* dollars a day.

The belief in the United States is now widespread that free trade has not worked. A solid majority of the American people favors significant changes in U.S. trade policy. A poll conducted by Allstate/National Journal (2010) contained an extensive battery of questions on trade and U.S. manufacturing. It revealed strong public majorities against free trade. For example, 68 percent of respondents supported a policy requiring that "a certain percentage of every high-end manufactured product, such as automobiles, heavy machinery, and transportation equipment, sold in the United States be produced or assembled within the United States, even if that means higher prices for their products." Similarly, only 21 percent of respondents favored the pursuit of more free trade agreements, as opposed to 73 percent who favored either tariffs or subsidies to strengthen America's competitive position.

Yet American policymakers and economists have been reluctant to take any action to balance trade. They have argued that the best response to mercantilism is a policy of unilateral free trade because mercantilism is a self-destructive strategy which eventually corrects itself. If they are wrong, then the obvious response to mercantilist-produced trade deficits would be a counter strategy which requires balanced trade, thereby blocking mercantilist attempts to produce trade surpluses.

KEYENS ON MERCANTILISM

The theory that mercantilism should be combated is not new. In the chapter about mercantilism from his magnum opus, Keynes (1936, 338) pointed out how destructive chronic trade deficits can be. He wrote that in certain situations:

> (A) favorable [trade] balance, provided it is not too large, will prove extremely stimulating; whilst an unfavorable balance may soon produce a state of persistent depression.

When Keynes wrote this, recent British experience was surely seared in his mind. In those days, France and the United States were the primary mercantilists. According to Keynes (1981, 600), by September 1931 the United States had accumulated half (one trillion pounds) and France had accumulated almost a fourth (£471 billion) of the world's gold stock. These two countries ran trade surpluses, while their victims, including Great Britain, ran trade deficits. Today China and other Asian countries are the primary mercantilists while the United States is the primary victim.

In 1925, when Britain returned to the gold standard with an overly high exchange rate after going off the gold standard during World War I, the United States and France both returned to the gold standard with overly low exchange rates. As a result, the United States and France experienced the "Roaring 20s," while Britain got mired in the recession that often envelops countries with trade deficits.

In order to buy more imports than they export, trade deficit countries must borrow from their trading partners or sell assets such as gold. At first their credit rating is good, but eventually they get so deeply into debt that they experience serious credit worthiness problems. The financial problems that follow years of trade deficits hit Britain in the early 1930s, just as they are now hitting many of today's trade deficit countries.

By 1931 in the addendum to what has come to be known as the "Macmillan Report," Keynes was advocating a system of tariffs on imports to be used to pay bounties on exports (Stamp 1931). His plan anticipated the Import Certificates plan proposed for the trade-deficit plagued United States by Warren Buffett in 2003. But almost before the ink was dry, events made the tariffs unnecessary. The British treasury ran out of gold and was forced to go off the gold standard on September 21, 1931. As a result, the pound fell rapidly against the French franc and the U.S. dollar.

Keynes (1982, 4–5) followed the statistics carefully, and was thrilled to find that, in the months following the devaluation, there was nary a problem. Britain's unemployment rate went down. Little inflation occurred because the prices of most of the raw materials that British factories purchased went down with the international price of the pound. Meanwhile, prices in France and the United States, still on the gold-standard, remained high, allowing Britain to undercut their manufactures in world markets.

Keynes (1982, 17) was completely satisfied. He immediately dropped his tariff proposal and urged that a meeting be held among the members of the British Commonwealth to discuss creating a free trade area among themselves, using sterling (the British pound) as its trade-settlement currency.

In an article in *The Yale Review*, "The Prospects of the Sterling Exchanges," Keynes (1932, 446) explained his thinking. If the United States and France, the so-called "creditor countries," insisted on receiving payment in gold for their goods, then trade would proceed elsewhere and force their trade into balance. He wrote: "The creditors by leaving no other means of payment have, in effect, demanded that the debtors shall find some way of destroying these creditors' own trade balances."

And that's exactly what happened. The United States tried to restore its trade surpluses, but to no avail. In 1930, the Smoot-Hawley tariff replaced the slightly lower Fordney-McCumber tariff of the 1920s. And as 1933 proceeded, President Franklin Roosevelt went on a gold buying spree which drove down the dollar from $20.67 per ounce of gold to $35 per ounce of gold. Keynes called it, "the gold standard on the booze" (Skidelsky 2000, 185).

However, in 1933 Britain's Imperial Preference System went into effect. This created a duty-free zone within the British Commonwealth with high tariffs on countries outside of the Commonwealth, including the United States and France. With factories moving into Commonwealth countries to access markets, Britain quickly climbed out of the Great Depression.

Twentieth century world history might have been very different if Britain would have had the courage to force balanced trade years earlier. Eventually, mercantilism ruins the export markets for the trade surplus countries' products, damaging the international trading system. Balanced trade can grow forever, but mercantilism eventually produces financial crises when trade deficit countries can no longer continue to buy as many imports. When severe, like the ones that began in 1929 and 2008, these crises reduce world trade and cause worldwide depressions.

Modern Keynesians believe that Keynes urged all countries, whether trade surplus or deficit, to engage in deficit spending to get out of depressions. This is not true. Keynes never advocated that Britain engage in massive deficit spending to get out of the Great Depression. On the other hand, he did urge President Roosevelt to engage in such spending.

During World War II, Keynes foresaw that the post-war world could be one of growing trade and the harmony that comes from growing trade, if only mercantilism could be prevented. So he tried to create a post-war international institution that would keep trade balanced.

Even though he did not have an official position in the British government, he was so influential, as a consultant to the British Treasury Department, that he was chosen to be Britain's chief negotiator at the Bretton Woods conference which established the IMF. Volume 25 of his collected writings is full of his plans for the fund which was to enshrine balanced trade as its primary goal.

Under Keynes's proposals, the IMF would have been an "International Clearing Union" which would establish an international settlement currency and keep trade in balance. Trade surplus countries would have to take down their barriers to imports, stimulate their economies and/or make loans to trade deficit countries. In contrast, trade deficit countries would be allowed to use export subsidies, devaluations, import restrictions, and/or tariff barriers.

This book might not have been necessary had Keynes had his way. Unfortunately Keynes was opposed at every turn of the Bretton Woods negotiations by chief U.S. negotiator Harry Dexter White, a Soviet spy in the U.S. Treasury Department who may have wished to weaken the trade-deficit Britain so as to bring about a U.S.–Soviet partnership after World War II. White's counter-proposal for an *International Stabilization Fund* became the basis for the IMF.

If Keynes's plan had been enacted instead, the financial crisis that triggered the 2008 recession could have been avoided. It began when the 1998–2006 house price bubble popped in the United States in 2006. Similar bubbles fed by mercantilist loans were occurring in other trade deficit countries as well. As in the 1930s, the crisis in the world economy was brought about by countries practicing mercantilism.

MERCANTILISM IS A PROBLEM

Economists have been slow to come to grips with the modern version of mercantilism. Take Nobel Prize-winning trade economist Paul Krugman, for example. The only reference to mercantilism in his 2000 textbook written with Maurice Obstfeld on international economics (Krugman and Obstfeld 2000) is found in a box on page 542 entitled "Hume versus the Mercantilists." The mercantilists of the sixteenth through eighteenth centuries believed that a country's wealth depended on its accumulation of gold which required a surplus of exports over imports.

According to Krugman and Obstfeld, "Hume's reasoning shows that a perpetual surplus is impossible." An inflow of gold drives up prices in the surplus country and drives prices down in the deficit country which tends to correct the trade imbalance. But Hume was wrong. If the goal of the gold mercantilists were to build their industry (not their gold hoard), they could have perpetuated mercantilism by lending the gold obtained from trade back to the trade deficit countries. Although in the long run some of this gold might have been lost (due to the ruined credit of the deficit countries), Krugman's (1987a) model of *learning by doing* shows that the end result would be productive, wealthy, and competitive economies among the mercantilists, and weakened, hollowed economies among their competitors.

According to Krugman and Obstfeld, the possibility of mercantilism under a system of flexible exchange rates is similarly impossible. The flow of foreign currency into the surplus country would tend to depreciate the currency of the deficit country, lowering prices in the deficit country relative to the surplus country and raising prices in the surplus country. But Krugman and Obstfeld were ignoring the strategy that the modern mercantilists have in fact been pursuing. They use the currency of the deficit countries to buy financial assets instead of gold assets from the deficit countries. They short-circuit the normal market correction long enough for serious changes in industry and comparative advantage to solidify. A decade later, Krugman (2010) reversed course, arguing that "right now we're in a world in which mercantilism works" and suggesting that the United States should threaten tariffs in order to force China to change course.

The consensus of most modern economists is that the mercantilists of the sixteenth through eighteenth centuries failed, a surprising conclusion given that the primary mercantilists (Britain, France, and Prussia) replaced their primary victims (Spain, Portugal, and the Dutch Republic) as economic powers.

The late University of Chicago professor Jacob Viner (1948), a student of economic history, came to a different conclusion. He delved into the mercantilists' writings and discovered a core theory which made economic sense. He laid out the twin goals of mercantilism as power and wealth and pointed out that the mercantilists thought these goals to be compatible, specifically:

> [P]ractically all mercantilists, whatever the period, country, or status of the particular individual, would have subscribed to all of the following propositions: (1) wealth is an absolutely essential means to power, whether for security or for aggression; (2) power is essential or valuable as a means to the acquisition or retention of wealth; (3) wealth and power are each proper ultimate ends of national policy; (4) there is long-run harmony between these ends, although in particular circumstances it may be necessary for a time to make economic sacrifices in the interest of military security and therefore also of long-run prosperity. (p. 10)

In order to accomplish these ends the mercantilist country places tariffs (and other barriers) upon foreign products while at the same time buying foreign assets (mainly interest-bearing bonds today; gold in the past). In other words, mercantilist governments maximize their power and their people's future consumption through the combination of import barriers and foreign asset purchases.

In an article published in an American economics journal, but ignored to their peril by the American economic profession (*Dynamic Analysis of the Viner Model of Mercantilism*), prominent Chinese economist Heng-fu Zou (1997) demonstrated mathematically that Viner's goals are compatible. At the time Zou was a World Bank senior economist. He is now dean of the China Economics and Management Academy at Central University in Beijing.

First, he found that the more present consumption that a mercantilist country was willing to sacrifice by accumulating foreign assets, the more power its government would gain and the more consumption its people would have in the long run. Zou (2011) reiterated this argument.

Second, he found that the more successfully a mercantilist government applied tariff barriers to foreign consumer products, the more it would gain in wealth and power and the more its people would gain in long-run consumption.

Zou did not address the effect of mercantilism upon trading partners. In fact, he assumed for the purposes of mathematical tractability that the mercantilist country was a small economy with little effect upon its trading partners. The actual effect upon the trading partner is exactly reciprocal to the effect upon the country practicing mercantilism. The trading partner gets increased consumption in the short run in return for reduced consumption and power in the long run. This effect is sometimes described in economics as the "Dutch Disease" based upon the observation that anything that increases a country's exchange rate leads to diminished competitiveness for its industries (Corden and Neary 1982; Ammendola 2011, 30).

History provides many examples of the costs of failing to respond effectively to mercantilism. For instance, the Dutch Republic practiced free trade in the face of mercantilism throughout the eighteenth century. First they lost their industries, then the foreign students at their universities, then their navy, then their stock companies, and finally their banks. In one century, they went from the richest and most technologically advanced country in Europe to one of the poorest. Here's how Edwin Way (2012, abstract) summarized what happened:

> The Dutch economy was by far the world's wealthiest and most technologically advanced as late as 1700, but subsequently experienced more than a century of economic decline as manifest in mass unemployment, rising inequality, an absolute decline in the median standard of living and a loss of technological leadership. The proximate cause of this decline was the evisceration of Dutch manufacturing, largely as a result of the systematic mercantilism that swept through much of Western Europe beginning in the 1690's. . . . Dutch elites . . . maintained largely unilateral free trade policies down to the Republic's final days.

Modern mercantilism is different, but the goal of running trade surpluses remains. The principal tool of modern mercantilism is the use of the savings of their countries to purchase foreign assets. The modern mercantilists buy financial assets, effectively lending their countries' savings to the world.

According to James Gagnon (2013, 3) of the Peterson Institute for International Economics, the diversion of savings by these foreign governments gave their countries trade surpluses, and thus gave the United States trade deficits. He illustrated this fact with a graph (his figure 1) which showed that foreign asset accumulations precisely corresponded in magnitude with current account surpluses (i.e., trade surpluses[1]) for these countries. He concluded:

> This paper finds that the large current account imbalances shown in figure 1 probably would not have occurred, and certainly would not have persisted, without massive official net purchases of foreign assets.

As a result of mercantilism, the United States got increased immediate consumption, especially since 2003. But the long-term effects have been entirely negative. As we will show in chapter 3, the American manufacturing sector declined due to lack of fixed investment, median incomes declined due to the loss of productive jobs in manufacturing and other trade-competing industries, and unemployment increased. Overall, the United States realizes unnecessary losses in comparative advantage and innovation that make it permanently poorer. Yet American policy leaders have done nothing that would stop this beggar-thy-neighbor mercantilism.

Take the Obama administration which took office at the beginning of 2009. Although President Obama imposed a few anti-dumping tariffs and filed a few World

Figure 1.2. U.S. Trade Balance with China

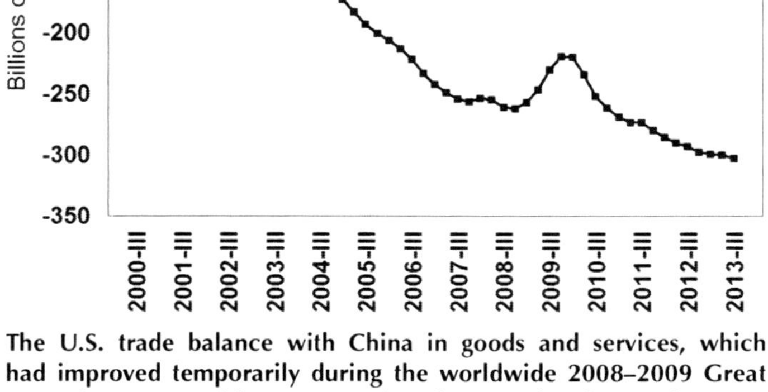

The U.S. trade balance with China in goods and services, which had improved temporarily during the worldwide 2008–2009 Great Recession, resumed its pre-recession downward trajectory in 2011. Source: BEA.

Trade Organization (WTO) complaints against China, none of his actions had any noticeable effect upon the U.S. trade balance with China which had improved temporarily during the worldwide 2008–2009 Great Recession but resumed its pre-recession trajectory in 2011.

During the Great Recession, the U.S. government let China engage in actions contrary to WTO rules, designed to ensure that factories closed, as a result of the worldwide downturn in demand, would be elsewhere. For example, on November 12, 2008, the *Financial Times* reported ("Tax rebates raised for Chinese exporters") that China would again raise its export subsidies on December 1, the third time since July (Dickie 2008). Meanwhile, the United States lost 1,600,000 manufacturing jobs from October 2008 to October 2009.

Normally, when a country's economy is growing fast, its demand for imports grows faster than its trading partners' demand for its exports. But despite China's 7–10 percent growth rate, compared to the United States' 2–3 percent growth rate, the U.S. trade balance with China worsened. China was usually able to grow its surplus with the United States without violating World Trade Organization rules because, when China joined the World Trade Organization in December 2001, it was given the status of an emerging market country which allowed it to keep tariffs in place, to apply tariffs to strategic sectors (including vehicles), and to impose tariffs to protect "infant industries." (Almost every industry in China is considered to be an infant industry.)

When President Obama campaigned for the presidency in 2008, he promised to take on China's currency manipulations. Here is an exchange from the final presidential debate with McCain:

> *OBAMA:* (W)e should enforce rules against China manipulating its currency to make our exports more expensive and their exports to us cheaper. . . . We've got to have a president who is going to be advocating on behalf of American businesses and American workers and I make no apology for that.
>
> *SCHIEFFER:* Senator?
>
> *MCCAIN:* . . . Now, on the subject of free trade agreements. I am a free trader. And I need—we need to have education and training programs for displaced workers that work, going to our community colleges.

Obama was promising to take on China's currency manipulations if elected president. McCain was promising to re-educate unemployed manufacturing workers at community colleges for non-existent jobs. But, once elected, Obama adopted McCain's policy.

Obama chose Timothy Geithner to be his treasury secretary, who shared his position on trade policy with his mentor Lawrence Summers, the architect of Obama's "recovery plan" (Geithner 2007). Both Geithner and Summers believed that the main trade challenge for the United States was convincing the American people of the benefits of globalization despite losses of manufacturing employment.

Summers planned to revive the economy through an eight hundred billion dollars plan using money to be borrowed from abroad, so Obama dispatched Secretary of State Hillary Clinton to China, not to insist on trade balance, but to beg the Chinese government for loans. The *Taipei Times* reported on February 23, 2009 ("Keep buying US Treasury bills, Clinton urges China"): "In Beijing, [Clinton] called on Chinese authorities to continue buying U.S. Treasuries, saying it would help jump-start the U.S. economy and stimulate imports of Chinese goods."

In the second quarter of 2010, Summers's "recovery summer" failed to materialize due to falling net exports. Summers had successfully engineered a simultaneous increase in consumption (C), business fixed investment (I), and government purchases (G), based upon the economic equation that:

$$GDP = C + I + G + \text{net exports}$$

Unfortunately, he ignored net exports (exports minus imports), and there went his recovery! During the second quarter of 2010, the supposed "recovery summer," C + I + G increased at a recovery-inducing 6.2 percent rate, but falling net exports (i.e., the rising trade deficit) reduced GDP growth to a 3.8 percent rate as shown in figure 1.3.

Figure 1.3. Why Recovery Summer Failed

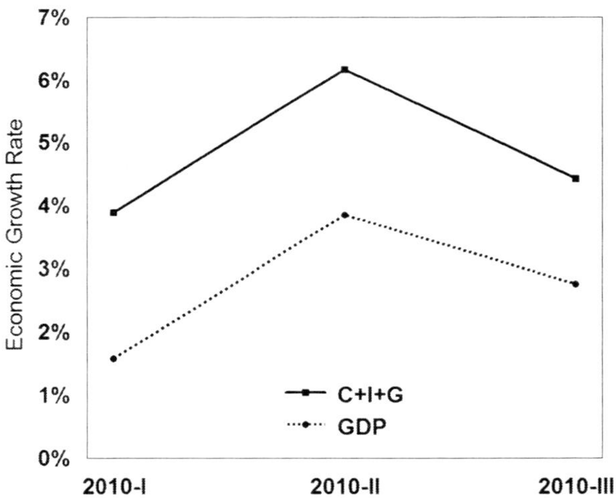

If the trade deficit had not changed, the real growth rate, shown by the solid line (labeled C + I + G), would have peaked at a 6.2 percent annualized rate in the second quarter, but due to the growing trade deficit, the actual growth rate, shown by the dotted line (labeled GDP), only peaked at a 3.8 percent annualized rate. Source: BEA.

When Lawrence Summers read the unemployment and GDP reports, he probably realized that the rising trade deficit was preventing the rapid U.S. economic recovery that he had engineered. So on September 4, he left for China to persuade the Chinese government to loosen its currency manipulations and other trade manipulations.

In anticipation of the meeting, the Chinese government erected a wall. They claimed that they don't keep their people from buying U.S. products. They claimed that if the United States just sold them the high tech gear that their military desired, trade would move toward balance. They claimed that their manipulation of the yuan-dollar exchange rate is an internal Chinese issue. Here is a selection from an Associated Press report from September 7 ("China rejects pressure amid US visit"):

> China rejected pressure over currency Tuesday amid a visit by two high-level U.S. envoys, saying Beijing will set the pace of exchange rate reforms. . . .
>
> The issue is expected to be on the agenda for talks between Chinese officials and the visiting director of the U.S. National Economic Council, Lawrence Summers, and Deputy National Security Adviser Thomas Donilon.

Although they rejected his requests, the Chinese government gave Summers a royal reception. Instead of being shunted to lower-level aids, according to a September 7 Reuters report ("China-US ties improving Hu tells White House team"), he met with China's President Hu Jintao and with the head of the People's Bank of China Zhou Xiaochuan. The Chinese went out of their way to achieve an atmosphere of friendliness.

That was Summers farewell tour. On September 21, he and President Obama held a press conference where they jointly announced Summers's resignation so that he could return to academic life, once Obama had found a replacement.

China is not the only mercantilist. South Korea, for example, like China, has accumulated foreign reserves in order to produce trade surpluses. The Federal Reserve reported that South Korea spent 4.24 percent of its GDP on foreign reserves accumulation between September 2009 and September 2010 (see figure 6.1).

Nevertheless, in 2012 Congress ratified and President Obama signed a "free trade" agreement with South Korea that did not require balanced trade. The agreement went into effect in March 2012. Immediately, the U.S. trade balance with South Korea (goods plus services) deteriorated, descending from a negative $6.4 billion for the year ending with the first quarter of 2012 to a negative $12.6 billion for the year ending with the third quarter of 2013 as shown in figure 1.4.

In 2013, President Obama's administration was busy negotiating so-called "free trade" agreements, modeled after the "successful" South Korea agreement. These agreements were to include many of the Asian and European trade surplus countries, yet none of them were to give parties with overall trade deficits the right to impose trade-balancing tariffs.

The United States is a principled nation which believes in the mutual benefits stemming from free trade. But the United States is giving other countries the

Figure 1.4. U.S. Trade Balance with South Korea

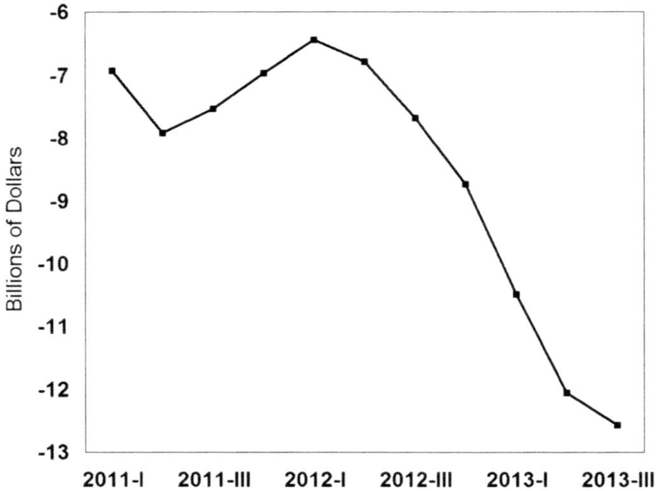

The U.S. trade balance in goods and services with South Korea began falling as soon as the U.S.-Korea Free Trade Agreement was passed in March 2012, at the end of the first quarter "2012-I" in the graph. Source: BEA

advantage by doing so. It is high time to combat mercantilism. Indeed the fear is that time is on the verge of running out.

NOTE

1. The current account balance is not precisely the same as the trade balance. Its main component is the trade balance, so, usually, when one is in surplus the other is in surplus and when one is in deficit the other is in deficit. Its other components are foreign income and foreign gifts.

2

The Problem of Private Savings Flows

The bewildered politicians of the southern euro-zone kept trying to reduce their high unemployment rates, but nothing that they did worked. First they tried stimulating their economies through massive budget deficits, but that just produced government insolvencies and higher unemployment rates. Then they tried to fix government insolvencies through austerity, but that just increased unemployment more.

The euro-zone economic problems were a chief topic of discussion at the May 2012 G8 summit of world leaders. President Obama called for the near-bankrupt governments to spend more on infrastructure. German Chancellor Merkel called on them to reduce their budget deficits (and thus their borrowing from Germany). Neither leader proposed anything that would reduce their sky-high unemployment rates. What would help these countries most would be a major shift in their balance of trade.

Figure 2.1 plots the 2011 jobless rates and trade balances (as a percentage of GDP) of the large euro-zone countries excepting Ireland. The trade-deficit countries in the left half (France, Finland, Greece, Italy, Portugal, and Spain) had higher unemployment rates than the trade-surplus countries in the right half (Austria, Belgium, Germany, and Netherlands).

This is not surprising; trade surpluses add to aggregate demand, while trade deficits subtract. Also, when a country has structural trade deficits, attempts to stimulate demand through profligate government spending leak abroad because imports increase without a corresponding increase in exports, and the added debt from government borrowing is difficult to finance because of already high debt. By continually paying more for imports than they get for their exports, they gradually run out of euros, just as trade deficit countries under a gold standard would run out of gold. Loans from the northern European countries perpetuate the problem without solving it.

Figure 2.1. Euro-zone Jobless Rates and Trade Balances in 2011

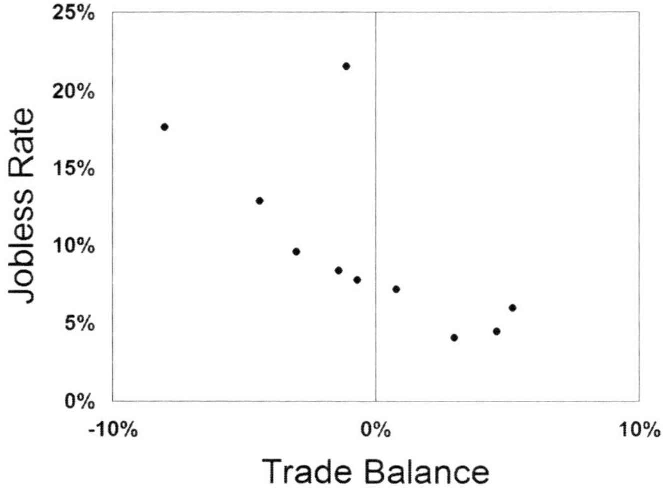

The trade deficit countries in the left half of the plot had higher jobless rates than the trade surplus countries in the right half. All countries with GDPs larger than $100 billion are shown except Ireland (jobless rate 15 percent; trade balance 22 percent). Trade balance (goods plus services) is shown as a percentage of GDP. Source: OECD.

Austerity (moving government budgets toward balance) might perhaps restore the ability of the trade deficit governments to borrow at low interest rates, but it only addresses trade deficits to the extent that it lowers wage rates and to the extent that lower wages lead to business investment in new production.

Although part of the euro-zone problem was mercantilist savings flows from outside the zone, the high unemployment was largely brought about by differences in savings rates within the zone. When euro-zone integration led to more equal interest rates, northern Europeans saved and southern Europeans spent. Perhaps northern climates, with their forbidding winters, tend to develop cultures that save for hard times, or perhaps Max Weber's "Protestant Work Ethic" is still in force even for countries where religion seems to have lost much of its power in public life, or perhaps the differences reflected different population age distributions.[1] Whatever the reason, with interest rates about the same across the euro-zone due to financial integration, northern Europeans tended to save more than southern Europeans, and, inevitably, the northern Europeans loaned money to the southern Europeans so that the southern Europeans could buy the northern products.

The savings flows from north to south for a time seemed to produce conditions of prosperity throughout the continent. Southern European economies boomed as inexpensive loans fed housing and other non-tradable investment and consumption.

Northern European economies boomed due to their trade surpluses. But the overall boom did not last. According to the Organization for Economic Cooperation and Development (OECD), the euro-zone was on track for its second year in a row of negative GDP growth in 2013 (OECD 2013, 12).

Milton Friedman, one of our [Raymond's] mentors, predicted these challenges at the time the euro-zone began. He recognized that a condition of the euros longevity was that each member had to earn as many euros (or as much foreign exchange that could be converted into euros) as it spent. Not necessarily every year, but the deficit could not go on indefinitely. Friedman pointed out that the euro is even less flexible than a gold standard because, under a gold standard, countries could still devalue their currency. But under the euro standard they were completely stuck. In an interview (Hawkins 2003), he said:

> We're in the midst of a wonderful natural experiment. You have a really different arrangement with the euro than we've ever had historically. We've had many cases in which a number of countries have used the same currency. That's when they've used gold or silver as money. But each individual country has been able to control the content of its own money. So while they were using the same commodity as currency, they were always in a position to determine what the terms of exchange were between their own currency and the other currencies.

Because the common currency removes some of the easier mechanisms for rebalancing trade, including currency devaluation, the main mechanisms left are migration and reduced wages.

WHY THE UNITED STATES GIVES FOREIGN SAVERS PREFERENCE

The euro-zone is not the only location where private savings flows have created enormous negative repercussions. In the United States, such flows have helped produce and sustain U.S. trade deficits, partly as a result of U.S. government policies that give foreign savers tax rates (0 percent) not available to most domestic savers.

In 1984 U.S. interest rates were very high. Donald T. Regan, U.S. Secretary of the Treasury, requested and received from Congress a seemingly minor policy change. Regan removed all remaining U.S. taxes on the interest earned by foreign investors. From the perspective of the trade deficit, this could make Regan the worst treasury secretary in U.S. history.

At Regan's request, the United States enacted one of the most foolish tax loopholes of all time, the private-foreign-savings tax loophole. Before 1984, most private foreign savers paid a withholding tax on any interest earned in the United States. They paid the United States a 30 percent rate of taxation on interest earned unless they were operating from a country that had a tax treaty with the United States which specified a lower rate.

Regan asked Congress to eliminate the 30 percent withholding tax in order to create a new tax loophole just for private foreign savers. After the loophole, they paid nothing, so long as their investments were purely financial, and not direct. We would not object if Regan had asked Congress to encourage foreign direct investments, such as the building of new factories in the United States. Direct investments benefit the U.S. economy; financial investments just bid down interest rates and bid up existing stocks and bonds.

Regan was not entirely to blame for this loophole; earlier secretaries of the treasury had negotiated tax treaties that were just as foolish. The removal of the withholding tax concluded a process that had been going on for decades: the reduction of U.S. government taxation upon foreign investment income earned in the United States. Why foreigners should be treated to exemptions not given to American citizens escapes us.

Tax treaties exist to resolve the potential for double taxation of income earned on foreign investments. Given their sovereign power over their citizens, some governments tax their citizens on their income wherever earned while others tax their citizens only on income earned domestically, excluding income earned elsewhere. From the enactment of the U.S. income tax, the United States has been in the first category but has allowed a credit on income taxes paid to foreign governments.

In 1919, the International Chamber of Commerce of the United States endorsed the credit for foreign taxes as a measure that all governments should adopt. It called on the League of Nations to take measures to eliminate the "evils of double taxation" (Carroll 1978, 53). That was a very sensible proposal but unnecessary in that U.S. companies operating abroad were already sufficiently served by the U.S. government's unilateral action of allowing a credit for foreign taxes paid.

In 1939, Sweden became the first country to unilaterally exempt interest earned by foreigners from taxation. After World War II, several other European countries followed suit in an attempt to attract foreign loans to help with postwar rebuilding. The treaty negotiated by the United States and the United Kingdom in 1945 provided for reciprocal exemption of interest on bonds and royalties at the source. As a result, when the Soviet Union later wanted to earn interest on its dollar reserves, it put those dollars in British banks. The British banks could then loan the same money to Americans without having to pay any tax to the United States on interest earned. As the United States negotiated similar treaties with other European countries, similar accounts were established in banks throughout Europe. These accounts were increasingly funded by private individuals who wanted to lend dollars to Americans tax free. The resulting dollar-denominated bank deposits in European banks came to be called "eurodollars."

The U.S. treaty with the Dutch in 1948 allowed the exemption of interest, royalties, and dividends at the source, but was later amended to permit a 15 percent tax on dividends. In 1955 the treaty with the Dutch was extended to include Dutch territories, including the Netherlands Antilles (NA), which ended up opening up a huge tax loophole in which U.S. corporations would locate a subsidiary in the

Netherlands Antilles for the purpose of borrowing money free of U.S. tax (their tax liability to the Antilles would just be 1 percent). Many treaty shoppers and tax cheats also took advantage of the tax loophole opened by this treaty, as pointed out by Giuseppe Ammendola (1994, 24) in his appropriately titled book about the 1984 tax loophole: *From Creditor to Debtor: The U.S. Pursuit of Foreign Capital—The Case of the Repeal of the Withholding Tax*:

> The U.S./NA Treaty was not just used by legitimate residents of the two countries or by third country investors who practiced treaty-shopping. It is widely assumed that many U.S. citizens used the benefits provided by the U.S./NA treaty to circumvent U.S. tax laws. The mechanism was similar to one used by third-country residents. The only difference was that the U.S. citizen would set up a shell company in a tax haven country protected by stringent bank and legal secrecy laws. From there the shell company would establish a Netherlands Antilles finance subsidiary and take full advantage of the benefits for residents provided by the U.S./NA treaty. The existence of another layer (the non-treaty tax haven country) would render any IRS investigative effort more arduous.

Even so, in 1984 exempting interest at the source was the exception not the rule. Almost all of U.S. tax treaties permitted the taxation of interest levied by the source country, albeit at fixed rates of 15 percent or less. The exceptional treaties should have been renegotiated to close the loopholes that they had created for tax cheats and treaty shoppers, but instead, in 1984 at the behest of Secretary Regan, Congress unilaterally expanded the tax loophole so that all nonresident foreigners, including foreign banks all over the world, could receive tax-free interest income from the United States.

The United States currently has tax treaties with over sixty foreign governments. Although most U.S. treaties are negotiated by the Secretary of State, tax treaties are negotiated by the Secretary of the Treasury. Almost all of U.S. tax treaties provide that they can be terminated unilaterally by either country. As a result, they are very easy to renegotiate and are often renegotiated. Less than one-third of current U.S. treaties have remained unchanged since 1983.

So why did the United States enact this tax loophole? There were two reasons. One was to help American banks compete with European banks in the growing eurodollar market. Regan figured that if the United States offered tax-free interest, those putting their money into the eurodollar market to avoid taxes would switch to American banks. His plan, however, did not end the eurodollar market, which instead kept growing, partly fed by Americans who illegally earn tax free interest by depositing their money in foreign banks and by foreign governments wishing to avoid the possibility of having their reserves frozen should they come into conflict with the United States.

There was, and still is, a simple way to end the eurodollar market. Simply terminate or renegotiate all tax treaties and reinstate the withholding tax on interest paid to foreigners. Bob McIntyre of Citizens for Tax Justice urged that the Netherlands Antilles tax treaty be terminated at a U.S. House of Representatives (1984) hearing on the proposed tax loophole to remove the withholding tax. Without the benefit of hindsight, he made a completely accurate prediction, specifically:

> [B]y discouraging foreigners from buying our goods, as the current approach does by making investments in our assets more attractive, we have contributed substantially to our enormous trade deficit and cost thousands of Americans their jobs in export- and import-sensitive industries. . . . [W]e will soon move into a position of being a net international debtor—along the lines of Third World countries. (U.S. House of Representatives, 238)

McIntyre's prediction that the United States would soon be a net international debtor came true in 1986. He was not the only one at the 1984 hearings who warned that Regan's proposal would strengthen the dollar which would cause increased trade deficits. Roberto C. Mendoza of Morgan Guaranty Trust stated:

> Among all the evidence that we have heard today, no one has disputed the fact that [this proposal] would strengthen the dollar. The only question is by how much. (U.S. House of Representatives, 244)

Regan ignored the warnings of McIntyre and Mendoza because he wanted to entice foreign savings so that the budget deficits produced by President Reagan's tax cuts would not cause higher interest rates which could crowd out private investment. He created a long-term economic problem for the United States (trade deficits) in order to achieve a short-term policy aim.

The loophole went into effect on July 19, 1984, and was still in effect when this book was being written. By taxing foreign investors at a lower rate (0 percent) relative to most American investors, the removal of the withholding tax creates a perverse incentive for Americans to depend upon foreign saving rather than saving themselves. It seems likely that this policy of favoring foreign savers has contributed to the decline of the U.S. savings rate from more than 10 percent from the 1960s through early 1980s to less than 5 percent in recent years.

THE FREE MOVEMENT OF FINANCIAL CAPITAL IDEOLOGY

The U.S. Treasury secretaries that followed Regan ratified his tax loophole by writing new tax treaties with foreign governments in such a manner that the United States would not tax their citizens' interest earnings in the United States while they would not tax American earnings in their countries. They adopted, as a philosophy, a radical version of the free trade ideology, that the flow of financial capital between countries (which causes trade deficits) should go untaxed just as the flow of goods between countries should be free from tariffs.

In 1997, the Pacific Rim countries known as the " Asian Tigers" discovered just how destructive the free flow of financial capital between countries can be. First speculative capital flowed into their countries which bid up their stock markets and other assets, raising the exchange rate of their currencies. What became known as the Asian miracle attracted foreign private speculators to invest in Asian stocks and bonds. The inflow of foreign capital led to stock market and real estate bubbles. Their bankers found it advantageous to borrow U.S. dollars from foreign banks at rates much lower than domestic interest rates and then lend those dollars for the purchase of real estate and securities. Banks in Japan, Europe, and North America became major creditors of institutions in Thailand, South Korea, and Indonesia, and the obligations were for the most part payable in dollars.

The bubbles started to pop on July 2, 1997, when Thailand was forced to allow its currency, the baht, which had been pegged at a rate of twenty-five baht to one U.S. dollar, to engage in a free fall against the dollar. Others, too, had pegged their currencies to the dollar. The flight of foreign capital caused a collapse in real estate and security prices. The Thai stock market registered a collapse of 15 percent in just one day. Besides Thailand, the economies of Indonesia, South Korea, and other Asian countries fell into depression. The fall in the exchange rate made the dollar obligations too onerous and the tigers had to default on their obligations.

The crisis has not been forgotten, even though the economies of Indonesia and South Korea rebounded in short order. In 2006, Thailand followed the example of Malaysia and imposed controls on the withdrawal of foreign investment. Most of the Asian Tiger governments immediately began accumulating dollars both in order to protect their currencies from future currency collapses and also in order to insure that their countries would experience trade surpluses, not deficits.

According to the free movement of capital theory, capital most efficiently moves to where it is most beneficial, absent any taxes or governmental interference. In line with this theory, Goulder (1990) conducted a simulation of the effects of a possible reinstatement of the U.S. withholding tax, the tax that had been eliminated by Regan's tax loophole in 1984. If foreign governments were to respond with their own taxes upon interest paid to Americans, he found, the result would be losses in U.S. residents' aggregate welfare as well as losses in global economic efficiency.

His simulations, however, were seriously flawed. They left out important effects that he discussed toward the end of his paper—the role of the withholding tax in curtailing tax fraud and the fact that many foreign governments still tax foreign savings. The actual effect of the 1984 removal of the withholding tax was to produce an artificial incentive, drawing capital to the United States where it would be completely tax free not only from U.S. taxes, but often from the countries where the capital originated.

Recently, economists have begun to discuss the growing empirical evidence that the flow of financial capital can be very detrimental to the country receiving that capital. Prasad, Rajan, and Subramanian (2007) found that the more a nonindustrial country was importing financial capital, the slower its growth. In their abstract they wrote, "Surprisingly, we find that there is a positive correlation between current account balances [the primary component of the current account balance is the trade balance] and growth among nonindustrial countries, implying that a reduced reliance on foreign capital is associated with higher growth." This was indeed a surprise to the many economists who still believe that financial capital benefits the recipient country. Prasad, Rajan, and Subramanian concluded that the deleterious effect of foreign capital is due to the resulting higher exchange rate that makes the recipient country's exports less competitive in world markets. They wrote:

> To summarize, we have presented evidence that capital inflows can result in overvaluation in nonindustrial countries and that overvaluation can hamper overall growth. To bolster this claim, we have shown that overvaluation particularly impinges on the growth of exportable industries. (p. 31)

Despite this strong empirical evidence that foreign financial capital hurts nonindustrial countries, they suggested that the inflow of financial capital may benefit industrialized countries such as the United States. But the private foreign savings tax loophole was detrimental to the United States for exactly the same reason that financial capital hurts non-industrialized countries. It strengthened the dollar and made U.S. products artificially less competitive in world markets.

More and more governments have recognized that controlling capital inflows is necessary in order to maintain prosperity. Chwieroth (2014, 70) begins a chapter about managing capital flows:

> Across much of East Asia, governments—concerned that a wave of inflows could generate instability—have recently introduced controls to restrict them. This is an interesting development. Until recently, the international financial community stigmatized such measures. As a result, governments, fearful of triggering an adverse reaction from official and private actors, refrained from introducing controls and thus saw their autonomy constrained. Now, the international community identifies controls on inflows as a legitimate policy instrument. For many observers the increasingly widespread use of these measures, and the international response to it, thus mark a significant departure from past practice.

An IMF staff paper (Ostry et al. 2011) even came up with a set of tools for governments to use in order to manage capital inflows. The tool kit included capital controls:

> Capital controls limit the rights of residents or non-residents to enter into capital transactions or to effect the transfers and payments associated with these transactions. Typical measures include taxes on flows from non-residents, unremunerated reserve requirements (URR) on such flows, or special licensing requirements and even outright limits or bans. (p. 11)

The idea that financial capital movement between countries *should* always go untaxed is foolish. There are times when countries should encourage that inflow through tax breaks (e.g., Europe when it needed loans for rebuilding after World War

II), but unless the inflow is being invested in ways that substantially strengthen their economies, trade deficit countries should do their utmost to prevent the net inflow of savings which causes and sustains their trade deficits.

The next chapter shows just how destructive the trade deficits have been for the United States and other countries. At the very least, when an excess of trade deficit causing private savings is entering a country, its government should tax those savings at the highest rates possible.

As this chapter and the previous chapter have argued, there is, on the whole, plenty of blame to go around for the U.S. trade deficits. The inflow of private foreign savings to a significant degree reflects deliberate U.S. government policies that incentivize and encourage foreign purchase of U.S. assets. American politicians and their advisors have chosen policies that accommodate and encourage over-consumption and under-saving. The resulting trade deficits reflect their policy choices.

Whatever the cause, the net inflow of foreign savings nearly always leads to trade deficits. We will discuss the significant short-term and long-term costs of trade deficits in chapter 3.

NOTE

1. For an examination of some theories about divergent savings rates in the euro-zone see Artus (2012).

3

The Problem of Trade Deficits

Whether caused by foreign governments (chapter 1) or by private savings flows (chapter 2), trade deficits impose a wide range of costs on countries that experience them. This chapter examines ways in which trade deficits increase debt, are associated with financial bubbles, cause unemployment, reduce median incomes, reduce investment in tradable sectors like manufacturing, and reduce innovation. These consequences have a longer term result that can permanently shift the terms of trade against the deficit country—the loss of comparative advantage in tradable sectors.

TRADE DEFICITS ADD TO FOREIGN DEBT

In order to buy more imports than they export, trade deficit countries borrow from abroad or sell assets, which adds to the net foreign debt (the value of a country's assets owned by foreigners minus the value of a country's and its citizens' foreign assets). The United States had no net foreign debt in 1985. Since then, U.S. trade deficits have gradually added to U.S. net foreign debt so that by 2012, as shown in figure 3.1, the U.S. net foreign debt had reached 24 percent of U.S. GDP. The United States had a larger dollar value of net foreign debt than any other country in the world in 2012.

Fortunately, despite the high U.S. trade deficits, the U.S. foreign debt has only been growing slowly. A key reason is that U.S. investments abroad are more profitable than foreign investments in the United States, perhaps in part because U.S. economic growth rates have been relatively low. Also, the U.S. tax code discourages American businesses from repatriating profits earned abroad, so American corporations have tended to reinvest their earnings abroad, compounding the profits.

Figure 3.1. U.S. Net Foreign Debt

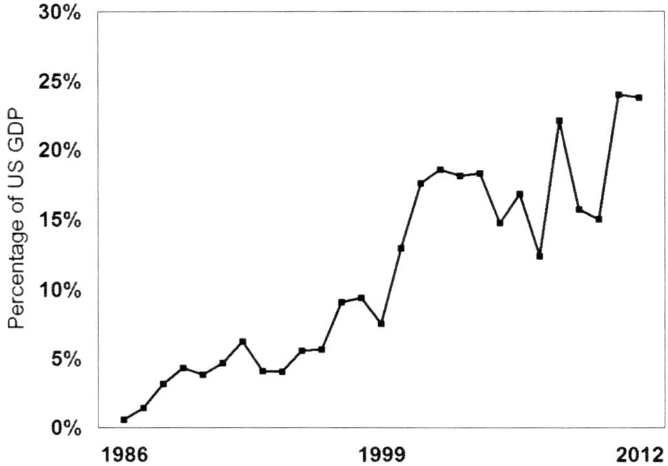

Since 1986, the U.S. net foreign debt has risen as a percentage of U.S. GDP. The net foreign debt (opposite of the *Net International Investment Position,* NIIP) is calculated by subtracting the value of American assets abroad from the value of foreign assets in the United States. Source: BEA.

The European trade-deficit countries have not had such good returns from their foreign investments and some have run much larger trade deficits. In 2012 Croatia, Cyprus, Greece, Hungary, Portugal, and Spain all had net foreign debt in excess of 80 percent of GDP (Eurostat 2014). In a report published by the International Monetary Fund, Reinhart and Rogoff (2013) pointed out that large overhanging debts tend to cause decades of slower economic growth. They recommended that advanced countries with large government and foreign debts consider either defaulting upon or inflating away their debts. When long term deficits produce enormous foreign debts, few other alternatives remain. Cyprus partially defaulted in 2013 when it expropriated a portion of the deposits in its banks.

TRADE DEFICITS AND FINANCIAL BUBBLES

On September 16, 2010, several monetarists with huge Republican-establishment credentials, proposed a solution to the U.S. economic malaise in an op-ed that took up nearly a full page in the *Wall Street Journal.* George P. Shultz (former treasury secretary), Michael J. Boskin (chair Council of Economic Advisors under George H. W. Bush), John F. Cogan (former deputy director of Management and Budget under

Reagan), Allan Meltzer (professor of economics at CMU and renowned expert on Federal Reserve history), and John B. Taylor (professor of economics at Stanford and undersecretary of the Treasury under George W. Bush), outlined their "Principles for Economic Revival" (Shultz et al. 2010). In general, it was an excellent exposition of fiscally conservative policies for economic recovery. Unfortunately, we do not think that what they proposed would work. The problem begins with their diagnosis.

Being monetarists, they held the belief that *if* the Federal Reserve would keep the money supply growing at a modest rate, *then* the economy would grow on an even keel. They blamed the Great Recession on the popping of the house price bubble in 2006, and they blamed the bubble on low interest rates, which they claimed were embraced by the Federal Reserve under chairmen Greenspan and Bernanke.

This was an unfair accusation. Until 2008, according to Federal Reserve and BEA statistics, the Federal Reserve under both leaders kept the brakes on money supply growth. In fact, during the 1998 though 2006 bubble, the Federal Reserve grew the narrow measure of money supply, M1 (which includes cash and checking accounts) slower (2.5 percent) than real GDP grew (3.2 percent). (The broader measure of money supply, M2, which includes money market accounts, grew at a 6.4 percent rate, about the same as the 5.4 percent growth in nominal GDP.) A U.S. monetary supply explanation also fails to account for the fact that the U.S. housing price bubble was not the only one. Many other countries experienced even larger increases in real housing prices during the post-1998 period. The low interest rates that fed the bubble were caused by the same influx of foreign savings that caused the U.S. trade deficits.

To evaluate whether countries with large trade deficits (as measured by the current account) had large housing bubbles (i.e., even bigger than the United States) while countries without current account deficits did not, we collected data on current account deficits from tradingeconomics.com for each of the twenty countries for which real housing price data is available from *The Economist.*[1] Figure 3.2 compares the current account deficits for countries with a large housing bubble with the current account deficits for countries without. A large housing bubble was defined as an appreciation in real house prices from 1998 to 2011 that exceeded the appreciation in housing prices experienced by the United States during that period.

The average 2007 current account balance for countries with a large housing bubble was a negative 2.84 percent of GDP, while the average current account balance for countries without a large housing bubble was a positive 7.19 percent of GDP. Thus, on average for these twenty countries, those with a housing bubble had a current account balance that was 10 percent of GDP worse. Apparently, the financial flows that sustained their trade deficits facilitated speculative over-investment in real estate.

Obviously untangling causality is extremely difficult here. Although the graph shows that there is a large relationship (and it is statistically significant $p < 0.01$), we cannot say for sure that the trade deficit caused the housing bubbles, as opposed to that the housing bubble caused the trade deficit.

Figure 3.2. Occurrence of Housing Bubbles

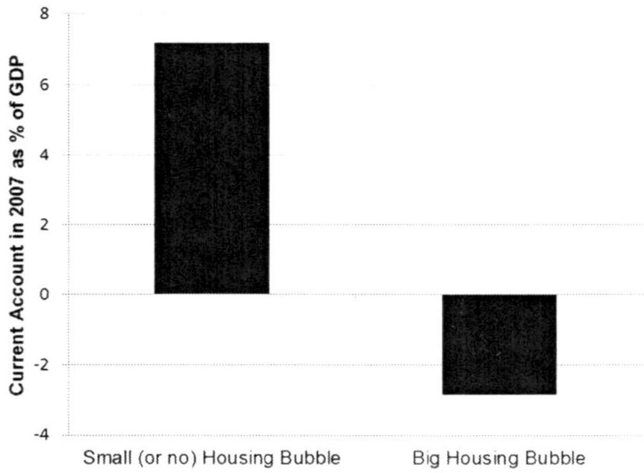

Countries with small or no housing bubble tended to have current account surpluses while countries with big housing bubbles tended to have current account deficits. The main component of the current account balance is the trade balance. As a result, current account balances tend to reflect trade balances. Sources: Economist.com and World Bank. Analysis by the authors.

One way to determine which causal story is correct is to look at the trade balances (as measured by the current account balances) before the housing bubbles were really rolling. In 2000 (before much of the appreciation in housing prices had occurred) there was already a large difference (4.65 percent of GDP) between the current account balances (as a percentage of GDP) of countries that later would have a large housing bubble and the current account balances of countries that would not. This difference is statistically significant at $p = 0.016$. This suggests that substantial current account deficits preceded and presaged the housing bubble, and suggests that they may well have caused it.

TRADE DEFICITS CAUSE UNEMPLOYMENT

Trade deficits also tend to have a pernicious effect on employment. As figure 3.3 shows, the average unemployment rate in 2011 for countries that had current account deficits in 2000 was much higher than for countries that had current account surpluses in 2000. Countries that borrowed and spent, later suffered when the loans came due.

For the sixty-five countries covered in figure 3.3 (all of the countries available on tradingeconomics.com for these particular years of data), the 2011 unemployment

Figure 3.3. Unemployment Rates Following Trade Deficits

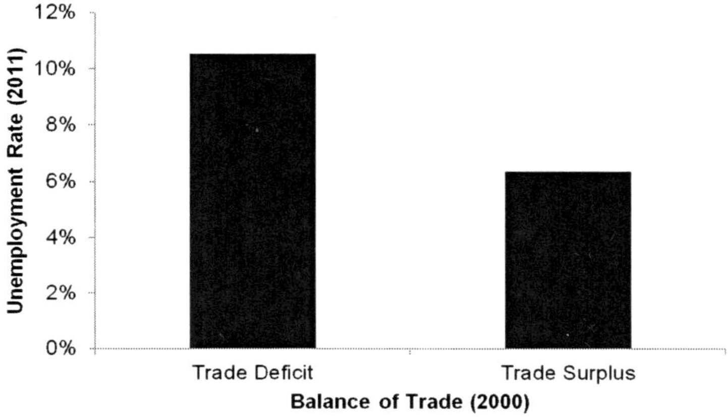

Eleven years afterwards, countries that had trade deficits in 2000 (as measured by the current account) had higher unemployment rates than countries that had trade surpluses. Source: World Bank data, analysis by the authors.

rate was nearly twice as large (10.7 versus 5.9) in countries that had a current account deficit in 2000, and this difference is statistically as well as substantively significant ($t = 3.4$, $p < 0.001$). In other words, a history of running deficits is associated with unemployment worldwide.

Trade deficits produce unemployment through direct and indirect routes. Consider the case of the United States. The direct consequence of trade deficits is that American producers face lower demand for goods than they otherwise would, while American consumers' income from their production does not match their consumption. With lower demand for American products, fewer workers are needed.

The Economic Policy Institute estimates that the U.S. trade deficit with China, alone, cost the United States 2.7 million jobs between 2001 and 2011 (Scott 2012). This reflects the hundreds of billions of dollars per year that would have been spent on American products had China used its import earnings to purchase American products instead of American debt. By buying U.S. debt instead of U.S. products, China deprived millions of workers of good jobs in export-oriented or import-competing industries.

In the long-term, financial flows that imbalance trade distort incentives. By altering exchange rates, they make costs in the trade deficit country higher, and costs in the trade surplus country lower. That encourages manufacturers in the trade deficit countries to build offshore, which diminishes the number of jobs in the trade deficit country relative to what they would have been without the trade deficit.

TRADE DEFICITS REDUCE MEDIAN INCOME

Unemployment is not the only problem that tends to afflict trade deficit countries. There is also the problem of declining median income because the productive (and thus well-paying) jobs lost in import-competing industries are not replaced by even more productive and thus better jobs in export-competing industries. Displaced workers are forced to accept jobs at reduced incomes.

Those in policy making positions in the United States should understand this, but most don't. For example, Gene Sperling (2005, 48), the lawyer that Obama picked to be his National Economic Advisor after Summers resigned, wrote in his 2005 book *The Pro-Growth Progressive: An Economic Strategy for Shared Prosperity*:

> When I lobbied for passage of trade agreements, I often explained that when a trade opening helped one hundred companies each create or save ten jobs, no one noticed the cumulative thousand jobs. Yet when a single company laid off one thousand employees, it was often a heartbreaking news story that shook confidence and caused anxiety far beyond the laid-off workers and their families.

Sperling was implicitly assuming trade balance—that jobs lost in import-competing industries would be compensated for by even better jobs in export-competing industries. However, U.S. trade was not balanced, so jobs lost were not compensated for by even better jobs. They were simply lost. The millions of jobs that would exist if China bought as much from the United States as the United States buys from China do not exist.

America's foremost trade economists have long understood Sperling's argument to be fallacious happy talk. Paul Samuelson (2004) took issue with frequent arguments by American economists that under free trade both trading partners necessarily benefit. This argument "is dead wrong about *necessary* surplus of winnings over losings—as I proved in my 'Little Nobel Lecture of 1972' and elsewhere" (p. 136). Samuelson continues that if trade leads to a gain in comparative advantage by the trading partner (e.g., through outsourcing of production know-how and tools), it can make a country worse off in absolute terms—its income and consumption declines.

Those who lose good-paying jobs in import-competing or exporting industries are often forced into taking less productive, and thus more poorly paid jobs in other sectors, if they can find any jobs at all. Largely as a result, since 2000, the growing trade deficits have been accompanied by a decline in median family income in the United States. The real median family income in the United States dropped from $55,985 in 2000 to $51,017 in 2012 as shown in figure 3.4.

TRADE DEFICITS REDUCE MANUFACTURING INVESTMENT

As a result of factories closing with few new factories being built, American workers have not been getting the new highly efficient tools that would make them ever more

Figure 3.4. Median Family Income

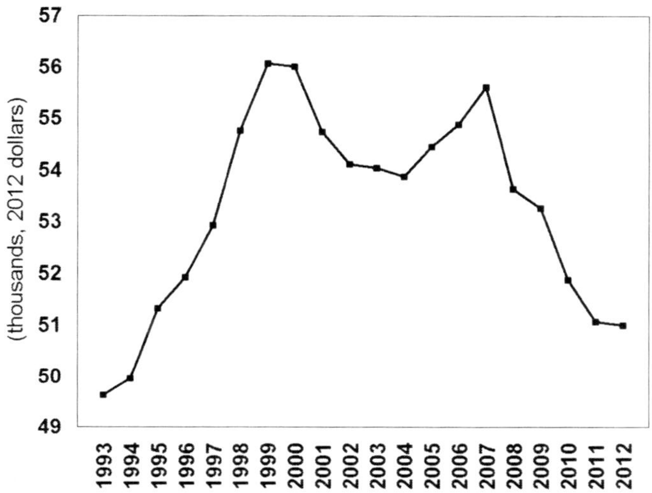

Real median income for American families has been declining since 1999. Sources: Median family income is from census.gov. Consumer Price Index is from bls.gov.

productive. In fact, American manufacturing employers have barely spent enough on equipment to replace tools and structures that were wearing out.

According to statistics released by the Bureau of Economic Analysis (BEA), net U.S. manufacturing investment (gross investment minus depreciation) averaged a minuscule 0.18 percent of GDP per year for the decade from 2002 through 2011, as shown in figure 3.5.

If the United States were trading other products for manufactured goods, the low manufacturing investment could be justified by jobs created in non-manufacturing tradables, but the collapse of American manufacturing investment coincided with the collapse in the overall U.S. trade balance for goods plus services.

Why is U.S. manufacturing investment so low? According to a careful study of 1987 business data by Chrinko et al. (1999), a 1 percent permanent reduction in interest rates and other investment costs should cause a 0.25 percent increase in the U.S. capital stock. Therefore, the savings sent to the United States by the mercantilist governments, which greatly reduced real long-term U.S. interest rates, should be increasing, not decreasing, net investment in U.S. manufacturing, a pattern exactly opposite to what has been observed.

We believe that savings inflows that support trade deficits cause diminished investment. One reason is that net savings inflows lower interest rates and raise exchange rates at the same time. American University economist Robert A. Blecker (2007) found that from 1995 to 2004, the rising exchange rate of the dollar proved to be

Figure 3.5. Net Manufacturing Investment

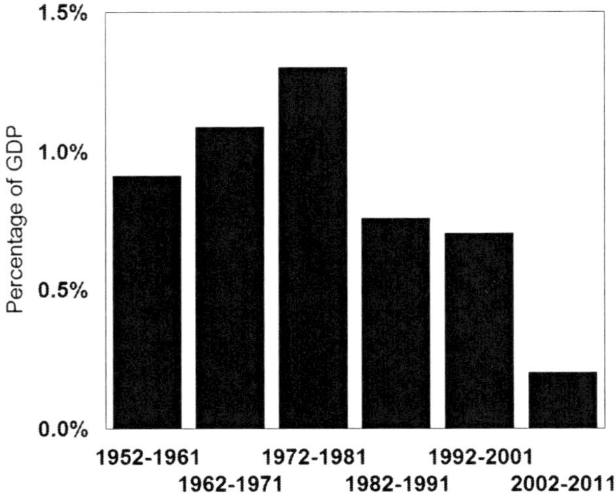

Net investment in American manufacturing (i.e., gross investment minus depreciation) has been declining. Source: BEA Tables 3.7ES, 3.6ES and 1.1.5, on August 16, 2012.

such a powerful factor against investment that it drove manufacturing investment downward, despite the fact that falling long-term interest rates were making capital goods less expensive.

Coupled with high exchange rates comes the lack of investment opportunities. Even when interest rates are extremely low, businesses will only invest where there are opportunities to make money. When mercantilist governments are the source of the savings flows that cause the trade deficits, they send their countries' savings to the United States in order to keep their exchange rates low, compared to the U.S. exchange rate. At the same time they often give their producers other advantages over American producers. As a result of such factors, foreign producers get investment opportunities, while American producers lose them.

The Chinese government keeps American factories from having the opportunity to sell in China through a wide variety of means. The simplest of which is government fiat. The Chinese government publishes catalogs of products that can be ordered by its huge government sector. Those catalogs simply exclude American-made products. And China also uses its state owned enterprises to exclude American products from Chinese markets. In testimony on March 30, 2011, before the U.S.–China Economic and Security Review Commission, Dr. Derek Scissors (2011), a senior fellow at the Heritage Foundation, explained one of its methods: "In most sectors [of China's economy], there is no market of 1.3 billion. Instead, there is what is left after the SOEs [State Owned Enterprises] are handed the bulk."

American manufacturers know that if they build their new factories in the United States, Chinese trade barriers will prevent them from selling to China. Moreover, mercantilism is slowing the growth rate in the United States and increasing the growth rate in China. If they want to sell to a rapidly growing market, they have to build their factories in China, where they are required to share their proprietary technologies with their Chinese partners and competitors.

Navarro and Autrey (2011, 80–82) explained the mechanism. In order to build factories that could sell in China, the Chinese government requires that foreign manufacturers form a joint venture with a Chinese partner, usually a state-owned enterprise. Also, the Chinese government requires that they share their intellectual property, not only with their Chinese partner but also with other Chinese producers. American companies have little choice.

Take General Motors, for example. Even while it was partially owned by the United States government (following the 2008 bailout) at the time, it was forced in 2011 and 2012 to build several new factories in China. In December 2011, a few American-made Cadillacs and Jeeps were getting over China's high 25 percent tariff barrier, so the Chinese government raised the barrier. According to a December 14, 2011, article in the *The Guardian*, China raised its tariffs on GM cars by as much as 22 percent and on Chrysler cars by as much as 15 percent:

> General Motors faces the greatest impact, almost 22 percent extra on some sports utility vehicles (SUVs) and other cars with engine capacities above 2.5 litres. Chrysler faces a 15 percent penalty, while a 2 percent levy will be imposed on BMW, whose US plants make many of the cars it exports to China.
>
> Existing taxes and duties already push up the cost of US imports by 25 percent, and the new levies make it even more expensive for Chinese consumers to buy American.

GM caved in April 2012 when it agreed to build several new Cadillac factories in China (Navarro and Autrey 2012). And by caving, GM was agreeing to share its Cadillac technologies with SAIC, a Chinese-government owned company that is both its Chinese partner and its competitor. Back on September 30, 2009, *Bloomberg News* reported that SAIC was already using GM's technology to produce cars for the Chinese market.

If the United States were to require trade reciprocity, then the Chinese government would no longer be able to force American companies to build their factories in China in order to sell in China. The Chinese government would be forced to let in imports from the United States, or its exports would have less access to the U.S. market. American companies would then be able to build factories in the United States, protect their technologies, and still sell to the growing Chinese market.

TRADE DEFICITS REDUCE INNOVATION

Trade surplus countries are not just getting the technologies that U.S. companies have developed in the past, they are also snuffing out future American innovation.

The unfortunate fact is that research and development (R&D) is best located near factories, as was made clear in a June 2011 *Report to the President on Ensuring American Leadership in Advanced Manufacturing* by the President's Council of Advisors on Science and Technology (2011).

The report just sought to reverse the decline in hi-tech manufacturing, not the decline in manufacturing in general. It dispelled many myths. For example, it rejected the commonly held misconception that the declines in U.S. manufacturing are simply due to wage rates being lower abroad:

> The loss of U.S. manufacturing leadership and jobs is not solely an issue of lower relative labor costs abroad. Strong evidence that labor costs are not the key factor is that the United States is lagging behind in driving innovation in manufacturing not just relative to low-wage nations, but also relative to nations such as Germany and Japan. Both countries make high-quality goods that command premiums in the marketplace. (p. 2)

It also rejected the idea that America can be a research and development country without factories. It pointed out that after factories move abroad, research and development often follow.

> R&D activity linked to manufacturing is moving offshore to access emerging global markets, and to respond to global competition for talent and the growing supply of scientists and engineers abroad. This is occurring as other countries are increasing their R&D intensities. Over the past several years, spending by U.S. firms on R&D outside the United States has grown at three times the rate of their domestic spending. (p. 5)

Without factories or R&D centers, Americans lose the infrastructure that stimulates innovations. Not only that, but they lose the kind of education that comes from learning by doing:

> [T]he United States no longer has the knowledge, skilled people, and supplier infrastructure required to produce light-emitting diodes for energy-efficient illumination, components for consumer electronic products like the Kindle e-reader, or advanced displays for TVs, computers, and handheld devices such as mobile phones. (p. 4)

In order to keep these innovations in the United States, the report recommended that the marginal rate of the U.S. corporate income tax be reduced, that an already-existing R&D tax credit be reworded so that it specifically applies to manufacturing R&D, and that five hundred million dollars be spent to encourage innovation by small businesses, modeled upon President Reagan's SEMATECH consortium which saved the American integrated circuit industry.

These are all good suggestions, but they all ignore the real problem of trade deficits that steal our industries. If the United States doesn't stop mercantilism, factories will continue to move abroad and R&D will continue to follow them abroad.

Ralph Gomory (2010b) lambasted Thomas Friedman, the well-known *New York Times* journalist and author, for arguing that the United States does not need to export manufactures, because it can export innovation instead. Gomory wrote:

> But the chasm-sized flaw in this otherwise alluring proposition is scale. Balancing trade on ideas and R&D simply cannot be done. The most elementary analysis shows that the scale is entirely wrong. As one who spent many years as the head of research of a large corporation, I know how much R&D matters; I also know how small it is. Eight percent is a very large percent of revenue to spend on R&D. Even in manufacturing, which is relatively R&D intensive, 4 to 5 percent is typical. It is really wrong to think that you can scale up R&D to be big enough so we can trade it for the huge quantity of things we need but don't make in this country.

Another flaw in this argument is even more basic. A report by the World Intellectual Property Organization (2013, 7) found that in 2012 China supplanted the United States in patents filed. "For the first time China holds the top positions for both destination and source of patent filings." If China is innovating more than the United States, then it is illogical to suppose that the United States can pay for imports from China through an edge in innovation.

LOSSES OF WHOLE INDUSTRIES OR OF COMPARATIVE ADVANTAGE

The classic model of trade assumes that comparative advantage is fixed. Each country trades what it produces with a comparative advantage for products that other countries produce with a comparative disadvantage. This especially makes sense when it comes to comparative advantage derived from natural resources but makes much less sense for complex manufactured goods in which comparative advantage develops over time, as firms learn how to produce goods more effectively.

When factories and technological advantages leave the United States, and thereby reduce or eliminate U.S. comparative advantage in those sectors, the result is diminished wealth in the long run. This is a central prediction of models of "learning by doing" innovation. Trade deficits imply that the tradable sector is not producing as much as it would if trade were balanced, and as a result this sector is less likely to incrementally innovate in ways that produce greater welfare and a stronger ability to supply world markets. Unless innovation proves to be very strong in the nontradable sector, the consequence is often diminished national welfare.

In a seminal paper, Nobel prize-winning economist Paul Krugman (1987a) showed that countries could use selective protection of infant industries to increase home wages (and diminish wages in their competitors) through capture of targeted industries. He also directly examined the consequences of currency misalignment, finding that transfer payments or savings flows that imbalance trade can have permanent negative repercussions for the recipient country.

> For a transfer of sufficiently long duration, all of the industries which move abroad in the short run will remain abroad even when the transfer ends. In either of the latter cases the home country's market share and relative wage will turn out to have been permanently reduced. (p. 50)

The loss of one industry can also have negative consequences for other industries as well. "External economies" from one industry can support others because there are almost always "knowledge spillovers." For instance, getting better at making computers has allowed the Chinese government to get better at making weapons, much more rapidly, moving into a competitive position where it is able to out-maneuver U.S. suppliers. Subsidizing one industry can have payoffs for other industries (Krugman 1987b).

Even leaving aside the important and intuitive concept of innovation resulting from previous activity in an area, there are other ways that trade deficits can lead to loss of industries and of revenue. Although it has sometimes been criticized because crucial results depend upon the mode of oligopolistic competition, the economic literature on "strategic trade" demonstrated that at times governments have an incentive to engage in policies that subsidize exporters, protect domestic markets, etcetera, in order to alter the terms of trade in favor of the domestic economy.[2] In other words, some of the time, non-free-trade or "strategic trade" policies allow governments to boost the national economy. Typically, though not always, this gain comes at the expense of other national economies.[3]

One version of the strategic trade model focuses on competition between firms in two countries to make sales to a third country. Because the market is not perfectly competitive, there are oligopoly profits to be made by the firm that makes the sale. If one country can distort the terms of competition (e.g., through a subsidy to its exporters or by driving up the value of the currency of the other country), it can drive the other country out of the market, and realize the profits all by itself (Krugman 1987b). These profits can, of themselves, repay the costs of the subsidy.

Arguably one of the reasons that "strategic trade" models have been less than robust is that they typically *assume* balanced trade. This forces countries pursuing market domination to trade off building strength in one industry against losses in another. Adding imbalanced trade removes this difficulty.

When manufacturing and innovation investment leave the United States, and when technological know-how and skills are outsourced, the result is often the reduction or destruction of what had been real U.S. comparative advantage. When U.S. companies and workers lack the skills, patents, and equipment to produce goods and services with greater relative efficiency the result is a diminished ability to command favorable terms of trade—diminished income. In the short term, these losses can be papered over by borrowing to consume—but in the long term the result is lower wages and diminished consumption.

The first presidential report to Congress on manufacturing, Alexander Hamilton's 1791 *Report on Manufactures*, shaped the growth of American manufacturing industry behind tariff barriers for the next 150 years. Manufacturing, even more than armed forces, won both World Wars and the Cold War.

Now, because the United States refuses to impose tariffs on foreign trade cheaters, it is thereby tolerating the dismantling of its manufacturing and other export sectors, the gradual impoverishment of the American household, and the gradual decline of new American innovation.

None of this is necessary. There is a basic economic principle involved. Balanced trade is way more important than free trade. When trade is in balance, neither country is "beggaring its neighbor," and neither country is accumulating potentially unsustainable debts. Balanced trade can grow forever, and forever benefit both countries involved. Countries that tolerate long-term trade deficits risk undermining their comparative advantages and impoverishing their peoples.

Why has the United States not effectively addressed the trade deficit? We will discuss the failures of economists, the political system and the Federal Reserve in the next three chapters.

NOTES

1. *The Economist* app allows the reader to compare nominal and real home prices across countries and over time. It can be accessed at: www.economist.com/blogs/freeexchange/2011/03/global_house_prices.
2. The initial statement of the strategic trade argument was by James A. Brander and Barbara J. Spencer, "Export Subsidies and International Market Share Rivalry," *Journal of International Economics* 18 (February 1985): 83–100. The article had about 900 citations in Google Scholar by June 2007.
3. For instance, by subsidizing Airbus, Europeans were able to increase competition in passenger airline production, driving prices down (which benefits European consumers among others). The subsidy also allowed Europe to capture a larger share of the aircraft market. For a more extended example, see Krugman (1987b).

II

THE FAILURES

4

The Failure of the Economists

Policies based on economic theories often become politicized and take on a life of their own. Those who disagree with them are "politically incorrect." Yet challenging accepted theories and proposing "better" theories is the very essence of the scientific method. In this book we challenge the accepted theory that free trade is always beneficial. Indeed we appear to be politically incorrect.

One of us (Raymond) broke with this conformist thinking in a commentary in the Pittsburgh *Tribune Review* (Richman 2003). He did not have to fear that he would lose out on publications, promotions, or research money because he had already retired. Another of us is tenured in a political science department. Political scientists, unlike economists, recognize that international relations involve the pursuit of power as well as prosperity. And we are not the only ones who have bucked the prevailing conformity. Many other economists are doing so, including Giuseppe Ammendola, Ian Fletcher, Ralph Gomory, Peter Morici, Peter Navarro, and Clyde Prestowitz.

THE FAILING CONSENSUS

Maurice Obstfeld (1995) published a much-cited work on the benefits of the free movement of capital. It was a fine mathematical model. It proved that free capital movement and globalization would benefit those countries that participated. Obstfeld's pro-globalization theme was echoed in a much-cited paper, "Trade, Growth, and Poverty" (Dollar and Kraay 2004), which found that the more poor countries engaged in global trade, the faster they grew. However, one of Dollar and Kraay's graphs showed that just the opposite had happened to rich countries. Even though they were participating more and more in trade as a percentage of their GDPs, their real per capita annual growth rates were declining:

- 1960s: 4.4 percent
- 1970s: 3.6 percent
- 1980s: 2.6 percent
- 1990s: 2.4 percent

And here's our calculation, using BEA and Census Department data, of real per capita GDP growth in the United States as it has participated more and more in trade:

- 1960s: 3.0 percent
- 1970s: 2.0 percent
- 1980s: 2.1 percent
- 1990s: 1.9 percent
- 2000s: 0.8 percent

But economists have rarely paid attention to this downward trend, perhaps because it didn't fit the beautiful theory. To their credit, Obstfeld and Rogoff (2009) acknowledged just how badly things had gone wrong, recognizing that global trade imbalances spurred by currency exchange interventions had contributed to the U.S. housing bubble and financial crisis.

In America today, despite the growing evidence that imbalanced free trade is not working, many American economists remain adamant in their promotion of free trade. They are also quick to label actions taken to balance trade as protectionism. For example, in 2007, 1,028 economists signed a petition sponsored by the Club for Growth (2007) against the United States taking any actions against China. It stated:

> As economists, we understand the vital and beneficial role that free trade plays in the world economy. Conversely, we believe that barriers to free trade destroy wealth and benefit no one in the long run. Because of these fundamental economic principles, we sign this letter to advise Congress against imposing retaliatory trade measures against China. . . .
>
> We urge Congress to discard any plans for increased protectionism, and instead urge lawmakers to work towards fostering stronger global economic ties through free trade.

Clyde Prestowitz (2011) pointed out that a claim, that combating mercantilism is protectionism, is simply ignorant:

> Just as the call for patriotism is often the last refuge of scoundrels, so the charge of "rising protectionism" is often the last desperate cry of globalists who don't understand that it is raw mercantilism that is turning their free trade dream into a nightmare.

In a world in which mercantilism is rampant, unilateral free trade is the economic equivalent of unilateral disarmament. Those that practice it are failing to recognize the reality of the world in which they live. They get short-term gains in consumption at the expense of long-term declines in power, economic growth, and future consumption.

The classical argument against mercantilism had three components: (1) the comparative advantage argument of David Ricardo, (2) the reduced consumption argument of Adam Smith, and (3) the market forces balance trade argument of David Hume. We will discuss these three arguments in turn, and show why they do not justify unilateral free trade in the face of mercantilism.

COMPARATIVE ADVANTAGE AND TRADE

Economists invariably "prove" the benefit of unilateral free trade with examples in which trade is in balance. They never consider what would be the effect of unilateral free trade upon a country running trade deficits that are intentionally caused by its trading partners.

When trade is balanced, we trade a basket of products that we produce with comparative advantage for a basket of products that others produce with comparative advantage and everybody benefits. But when trade is intentionally kept out of balance by mercantilist trading partners, they produce both what they can produce with comparative advantage and also what we can produce with comparative advantage and only import from us raw materials and products that are too costly for them to produce at home.

The advantages of international trade based on comparative advantage are clear. In 1821, David Ricardo (1911) summarized the case for free trade as follows:

> Under a system of perfectly free commerce, each country naturally devotes its capital and labour to such employments as are most beneficial to each. This pursuit of individual advantage is admirably connected with the universal good of the whole. By stimulating industry, by rewarding ingenuity, and by using most efficaciously the peculiar powers bestowed by nature, it distributes labour most effectively and most economically: while, by increasing the general mass of productions, it diffuses general benefit, and binds together, by one common tie of interest and intercourse, the universal society of nations throughout the civilized world. It is this principle which determines that wine shall be made in France and such as Portugal, that corn shall be grown in America and Poland, and that hardware and other goods shall be manufactured in England.

In this context, government interventions that distort market incentives are unambiguously bad. Normally when trade is balanced, jobs that are lost competing with imports are replaced by even more productive and better paying jobs producing exports. But when trade is kept imbalanced by country A, there are not as many jobs producing exports in country B. Country A's workers gain jobs and incomes, while country B's workers lose jobs and incomes. Country A gains industries and country B gains debt. In this context, there are fewer gains from trade for country B.

Matters are in fact worse than this, however. In many cases comparative advantage is not something fixed like the advantage that Portugal and France have with the production of wine in Ricardo's example. Comparative advantage in manufacturing is often based upon economies of scale. Country A can obtain country B's comparative advantage.

Among the relatively few economists who view the loss of American industry to foreign countries as a catastrophe in the making is Professor Ralph Gomory, research professor at the Stern School of Business at New York University and president emeritus of the Alfred P. Sloan Foundation. Professor Gomory is no ordinary academic; his PhD is in mathematics and he has a mathematical theorem named after him. He also made his mark as senior vice president for science and technology at IBM. He is the co-author with Professor William Baumol, distinguished former professor of economics at Princeton University, of a seminal work published in 2000, *Global Trade and Conflicting National Interests* (Gomory and Baumol 2000). They modeled international trade in a world in which countries can acquire a "comparative advantage" by specializing in any industry in which they can obtain economies of scale.

With acquired advantages playing a decisive role, Japan could specialize in autos and the United States in airplanes or Japan could specialize in airplanes, and the United States in autos. Who is first to achieve economies of scale in an industry is likely to continue specializing in that industry and give potential foreign competitors a high hurdle to overcome in order to compete successfully.

Gomory and Baumol showed that the realistic addition of acquired comparative advantage created potential conflicts of interest between trading partners even when trade is in balance. Improvements in the productivity of trading partners can lead to real declines in the standard of living. Failure to maintain comparative (e.g., technological or scale productivity) advantage in enough industries can make a country poorer, a point that is echoed by Samuelson (2004). Gomory and Baumol's analysis assumed balanced trade, but it is obvious that with imbalanced trade, the destruction of comparative advantage can proceed much more quickly (see Krugman 1987a).

Gomory (2010c) examined the consequences of trade intentionally kept out of balance by mercantilist trading partners.

> Our massive trade deficit is destroying significant segments of American industry and eliminating badly needed jobs. This is happening because we are slow to recognize an unpleasant reality: We do not live in a world of textbook free trade. We live in a world where our trading partner China has chosen mercantilism and is using the full powers of its government to advance its industries in ways that destroy ours. If we continue to turn a blind eye to this reality we will become a poor nation. However we can deal with our trade deficit; we can balance trade.

If one recognizes the fact that comparative advantage can sometimes be acquired, then running trade deficits is particularly problematic because it undermines economies of scale and takes away opportunities for learning by doing. Borrowing to finance consumption, as the United States has done, simultaneously increases future obligations (debt) and decreases future ability to pay (comparative advantage). The U.S. industries (e.g., electronics, computer hardware, pharmaceutical manufacture) that might perhaps have generated exports with which to pay debts and purchase future imports are weakened or no longer exist as a result of outsourcing. Professor Gomory's analysis suggests that large long-term trade deficits are a road to national economic suicide.

THE CONSUMERS VS. PRODUCERS ARGUMENT

Another argument brought up by those who favor unilateral free trade is that mercantilism hurts its own consumers and helps the consumers of its victims. Therefore, the United States should appreciate what mercantilists are doing for us. For example Harvard political economy professor Dani Rodrik (2013) argued that even though mercantilism works and is practiced by state-capitalist (fascist) governments, the liberal capitalist governments of the west should do nothing to oppose it. "Liberalism and mercantilism can coexist happily in the world economy. Liberals should be happy to have their consumption subsidized by mercantilists."

Rodrik was giving a version of the "consumers are hurt by mercantilism" argument of Adam Smith's (1776) classic, *The Wealth of Nations.* That argument helped end the era of mercantilism which dominated the economic policies of the European powers from the sixteenth through eighteenth centuries. Smith's chief claim was that mercantilism hurts the economy of the country practicing it because it hurts consumers in order to benefit producers. He wrote:

> Consumption is the sole end and purpose of all production; and the interest of the producer ought to be attended to only so far as it may be necessary for promoting that of the consumer. The maxim is so perfectly self-evident that it would be absurd to attempt to prove it. But in the mercantile system the interest of the consumer is almost constantly sacrificed to that of the producer; and it seems to consider production, and not consumption, as the ultimate end and object of all industry and commerce. (iv.8.49)

A rephrasing of this argument is the typical defense of free trade given by most economists when asked what they would do to reverse chronic trade deficits: "If your trading partner is foolish enough to ship goods to you in exchange for paper, why should you object?" Professor Milton Friedman said that to his students sixty years ago at the University of Chicago and Professor Allan Meltzer of Carnegie Mellon University wrote that to one of us in 2010.

The main trouble with this argument is that it is short-sighted. Although the victims of mercantilism do get *increased consumption* in the *short run*, they pay for that increased consumption with their industries and financial assets. In the *long-run* they get stagnant economies, financial crises, and *reduced consumption.*

Rodrik recognized that the liberal capitalist economies were in decline, but he appeared to be unaware that the decline could be predicted. As we pointed out, based upon modern mercantilist writing (Viner 1948; Zou 1997), the mercantilist country sacrifices some short-run consumption in order to get even more consumption and more power in the long run.[1] Conversely as we have pointed out (Richman, Richman, and Richman 2011), its victims get just the opposite: more consumption in the short run, followed by less consumption and power in the long-run. This scenario has already played out in at least three different trade deficit countries:

1. *Spain.* Spain's fellow European countries, especially Britain and France, stole Spain's industries and power through mercantilism in the sixteenth and seventeenth centuries.
2. *Dutch Republic.* British, French, and Prussian mercantilism stole Dutch industries during the eighteenth century, turning one of the richest countries of Europe into a relative pauper.
3. *Great Britain.* Britain eschewed mercantilism in the nineteenth and early twentieth centuries only to have its industries stolen by American and French mercantilism in the 1920s.
4. *United States.* After World War II, the United States eschewed mercantilism, only to have its industries and power stolen by Asian mercantilism from the 1950s to the present.

The "free lunch" of goods paid for with loans that mercantilists offer isn't free. In the long run its price is debt and poverty. If comparative advantage were static and debt could be costlessly repudiated, then Smith's argument might imply the conclusions that Friedman, Meltzer, and Rodrik want to draw.

MERCANTILISM CURES ITSELF ARGUMENT

Many economists assume that mercantilism is just a developmental strategy—that it will eventually be abandoned by its practitioners once they develop. They even call it an "export-led development strategy," as if restricting imports had anything to do with promoting exports. It is indeed a growth strategy, the strategy of growing one's economy at one's trading partners' expense!

It is true that mercantilists eventually abandon mercantilism. Mercantilism becomes pointless once their trading partners are too poor to be able to buy more imports than exports or once trading partners refuse to cooperate. Indeed Britain gave up mercantilism in the nineteenth century and the United States in the 1930s, after it stopped working.

But the fact that countries eventually give up mercantilism after destroying the economies of their trading partners is cold comfort to their trading partners. Spain never again was a world power, the Dutch never again led Europe in technology and trade, Britain is now a shadow of its former self, and the United States may never fully recover.

Furthermore, Japan may turn out to be a counter-example. In the mid-2000s, it appeared to be heading down the same path to free trade that Great Britain and the United States had taken. Even though it had grown to be a world economic powerhouse during the second half of the twentieth century through mercantilism, it was abandoning currency manipulations. But in 2013, it resumed accumulating foreign assets and fixing the dollar-yen exchange rate. Ambrose Evans-Pritchard (2013) wrote at the beginning of 2013:

> Japan's new premier Shenzo Abe is sweeping into office like Roosevelt in 1933, commanding the central bank to do whatever it takes to defeat deflation, deliver 3pc NGDP growth, and drive the dollar-yen rate to 90.

The argument that mercantilism is temporary began with the gold-flow theory presented by David Hume (1742) in part II of his *Essay on the Balance of Trade*, an essay that influenced Adam Smith's writing. Hume began:

> Can one imagine, that it had ever been possible, by any laws, or even by any art or industry, to have kept all the money in SPAIN, which the galleons have brought from the INDIES? Or that all commodities could be sold in FRANCE for a tenth of the price which they would yield on the other side of the PYRENEES, without finding their way thither, and draining from that immense treasure? What other reason, indeed, is there, why all nations, at present, gain in their trade with SPAIN and PORTUGAL; but because it is impossible to heap up money, more than any fluid, beyond its proper level? The sovereigns of these countries have shown, that they wanted not inclination to keep their gold and silver to themselves, had it been in any degree practicable. (ii.v.12)

According to this argument, imbalanced trade cannot long last under a gold standard. If a trade surplus country collects gold from its trade deficit trading partners, the increased money supply in the trade surplus country would cause its wages and prices to go up. Meanwhile, the reduction in the money supply in the trade deficit countries would cause their wages and prices to fall. The change in the relative costs of production would balance trade.

However, Hume never figured on the modern version of mercantilism in which the government of the mercantilist country stocks up on the currency of the trade deficit country and uses it to buy financial assets in the deficit country. These are acts which are appropriately called mercantilism because they are intended to perpetuate the surplus of exports over imports. They short-circuit the normal market correction no matter whether the world is on a gold standard or on a standard of freely traded currencies.

A modern version of Hume's argument holds that the capital inflows that accompany trade deficits benefit the country that receives the capital. When one country has higher returns on capital (i.e., higher interest rates), capital tends to flow into it. This capital will produce fixed investment, as did the inflow of capital to the United States during the nineteenth century or the inflow of capital that helped rebuild

Europe after World War II. The resulting economic growth makes up for the temporary trade deficits and balances trade in the long-run.

But while *private* capital indeed often flows to where it can obtain the highest return, *public* capital does not. Mercantilist governments buy foreign financial assets even when the rates of return on capital are higher in their own country than abroad. They even suppress their own people's access to credit in order to collect this capital and make loans abroad.

Foreign capital only makes an economic contribution to growth and employment when it is invested in new productive assets. The purchase of financial and existing assets instead leads to house or stock price bubbles or increased consumption of consumer goods, which provide only short-term benefit. Eventually, the loans must be paid back with interest even though they have already adversely affected the industries that compete in world markets where the wherewithal to repay must be earned.

Figure 4.1 illustrates this pattern in an analysis of all world economies running trade deficits or surpluses in excess of 5 percent of GDP. When countries run large current account deficits, they accumulate debt in one form or another. And this debt can later cause serious economic harm. The figure compares the growth rates of countries that ran large average current account deficits (more than 5 percent of GDP) and countries that ran large current account surpluses (more than 5 percent of GDP) from 2002 to 2007.

Figure 4.1. Relationship Between Trade Balances and Growth

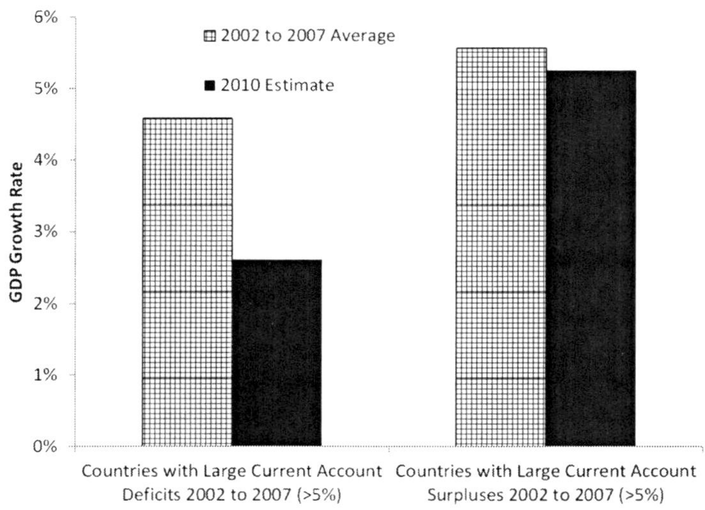

Countries that had large trade deficits (5 percent of GDP as measured by the current account from 2002 to 2007) had much slower growth during the 2002 to 2007 period and also during 2010 than countries with large trade surpluses. Source: IMF data; analysis by the authors.

From 2002 through 2007 there were differences—the average growth rate was higher for countries with surpluses. The differences were even more pronounced in the 2010 growth estimates. Countries with a history of running trade surpluses had recovered rapidly from the 2008 financial crisis and recession and were growing quickly. Countries with a history of running current account deficits had not.

In the case of the United States, the net loans associated with trade deficits have not provided investment benefits because they simultaneously lowered interest rates and took away investment opportunities. Foreign loans to the United States mainly financed consumer spending and a house price bubble, as we discussed in chapter 3.

CONCLUSION

In a world that is free of mercantilism, countries that practice free trade are better off than those that practice protectionism, because countries that practice protectionism hurt their consumers and sacrifice their other industries in order to favor the politically connected ones.

Although monetary mercantilism reduces short-term consumption, it increases long-term consumption and power in the mercantilist country. Meanwhile, it has the exact opposite effect upon its trading partners, giving them short-term gains in consumption combined with long-term losses in consumption and power. Furthermore, market mechanisms do not correct the resulting trade imbalances, nor do they compensate for the long term shift in production and consumption towards the mercantilist. Achieving the full benefits of international trade requires an effective response to mercantilism and imbalanced trade.

The case can be made even more broadly. Whether or not the trade imbalance with China is due to China's mercantilist practices—which we believe to be true—the cause does not matter. Whether you call it protectionism or not, policies intended to achieve balanced trade in the face of chronic deficits should be freely available. The policy our analysis supports is the Scaled Tariff, which we will discuss in chapter 9.

NOTE

1. The reduction in consumption may be so modest as to not at all be politically difficult to bear. A country that is rapidly transitioning from subsistence agriculture to manufacturing might experience 6 percent instead of 8 percent growth for instance. China has perhaps paid some short term cost in lost consumption due to mercantilism, but its people have seen their incomes double and redouble as the country has become a world leader in manufacturing.

5

The Failure of the Political System

Former Vice President Al Gore is able to explain things in the simple language used by elementary school teachers, so he tends to be believed even when he is conveying misinformation. In his 1993 NAFTA debate with Ross Perot, Gore claimed that the U.S. Smoot-Hawley Tariff Act caused the Great Depression of the 1930s worldwide. Holding up a photo of Senator Reed Smoot and Representative Willis C. Hawley, Gore said:

> We've also had a test of *his* [pointing to Ross Perot] theory. In 1930 when the proposal by Mr. Smoot and Mr. Hawley was to raise tariffs across-the-board to protect our workers, and I brought some pictures, too. This is a picture of Mr. Smoot and Mr. Hawley. They look like pretty good fellows. They sounded reasonable at the time. A lot of people believed them. The Congress passed the Smoot-Hawley protection bill. (*He* [pointing to Ross Perot] wants to raise tariffs on Mexico.) They raised tariffs, and it was one of the principal causes, many economists say *the* principal cause, of the Great Depression in this country and around the world.

It turns out that Perot, not Gore, was correct about Mexico and NAFTA. Mexico cheats through foreign currency purchases to keep the peso low and the dollar high, so that, despite NAFTA's tariff reductions, Mexican products are artificially inexpensive in the United States and U.S. products are artificially expensive in Mexico. Federal Reserve Chairman Ben Bernanke reported in a November 2010 speech (see figure 6.1) that between September 2009 and September 2010, the Mexican government devoted 3.64 percent of Mexico's GDP to foreign currency purchases.

Gore was also wrong in his implication that high tariffs first passed Congress due to the personal persuasiveness of Senator Smoot and Representative Hawley. The U.S. Constitution gives Congress the power to "collect Taxes, Duties, Imposts and Excises, to pay the Debts and provide for the common Defence and general

Welfare of the United States," and until the 1930s, Congress had leaned heavily on tariffs as a source of revenue. Tariff rates were set through lengthy deliberations in Congress, and typically responded to the balance of domestic local economic interests. From Washington's presidency to Smoot-Hawley, the United States had developed into a manufacturing powerhouse behind high tariff walls. Furthermore, the Smoot-Hawley tariff was only marginally higher than the tariff it replaced, the Fordney-McCumber tariff of 1922 which had contributed to the prosperous 1920s in the United States.

When Al Gore claimed that Smoot-Hawley was a mistake just because it was a tariff, he was mistaken. Smoot-Hawley was a mistake because the United States was a mercantilist trade surplus country with a billion dollar per year trade surplus pursuing policies aimed at beggaring its trading partners even in the midst of a global economic contraction. Smoot-Hawley failed because it goaded free-trade countries into fighting back against U.S. mercantilism. In 1932, in response to the Smoot-Hawley tariff, Great Britain established an "imperial preference" trading system with its colonies and independent dominions. The British engaged in free trade within their commonwealth while the entire commonwealth placed high tariffs on the rest of the world, including trade surplus countries such as the United States and France.

As a result, Great Britain quickly climbed out of the Great Depression. By April of 1934 it had exceeded pre-depression real GDP (Mitchell, Solumou and Weale 2009, figure 1). Trade deficit countries can exit recessions and depressions, as Great Britain did, by placing tariffs on the trade surplus countries and by increasing their trade with those countries that engage in balanced trade.

Today the roles are changed. China is now the primary mercantilist country and the United States is the primary victim. The United States could exit from economic stagnation by placing tariffs on the mercantilist countries and by trading more with countries that do not manipulate trade. But both parties, the Democrats and the Republicans, do worse than nothing. When they do take actions, they usually enable mercantilism.

A case in point was China's accession to the World Trade Organization in December 2001. It is rare when a government official actually blames himself for his own mistakes. That straight talk occurred in the June 4, 2008, issue of *Foreign Policy in Focus* when Robert Cassidy (2008), President Clinton's Assistant U.S. Trade Representative for Asia and China, took himself to task for the trade agreement he negotiated with China. He began:

> As the principal negotiator for the landmark market access agreement that led to China's accession to the World Trade Organization (WTO), I have reflected on whether the agreements we negotiated really lived up to our expectations. A sober reflection has led me to conclude that those trade agreements did not.

Cassidy noted that only two groups benefited from our trade agreement with China: "multinational companies that moved to China and the financial institutions that financed those investments, trade flows, and deficits." The American economy and the American worker were the big losers. Here is how he explained why his "free trade" recipe was flawed, even though he succeeded in reducing Chinese tariffs:

> China has adopted an *export-led development strategy* [italics ours], the centerpiece of which is a currency that is undervalued by 20–80 percent, with the consensus leaning toward 40 percent. Thus China's wages, in U.S. dollar terms, are 40 percent cheaper than they would have been if the currency were allowed to freely float. Similarly, foreign investors receive a 40 percent subsidy to develop operations in China. To add insult to injury, our exports are taxed at an additional effective 40 percent rate.

We would use the less-charitable term *mercantilism* to describe what Cassidy calls China's "export-led development strategy." The goal of an "export-led growth strategy" is to maximize exports; the goal of a mercantilist strategy is not only to maximize exports, but also to minimize imports.

Cassidy's "mea culpa" may have ruined his chances for a job with the Obama administration. Two of his unrepentant partners in the crime of negotiating this flawed agreement, Lawrence Summers and Gene Sperling, were successively chosen by Obama for his top economic advisor slot (National Economic Advisor), while Cassidy was relegated to the sidelines.

Neither major political party today offers anything approximating a sound position on U.S. international trade. Although both parties have individuals who understand the costs of unbalanced trade, the dominant faction in both parties supports the failing status quo. It is remarkable, and an indictment of American democracy, that both parties take such positions in spite of clear popular majorities for better policies.

DIVISIONS WITHIN THE DEMOCRATIC PARTY

President Obama and the Democratic Party have long been two-faced on the trade issue. During the 2008 presidential campaign Obama promised publicly that he would take on Chinese trade manipulations. However, behind closed doors, speaking to his outsourcing Silicon Valley campaign donors, he claimed that those who opposed Clinton and Bush's trade policy were racists and xenophobes bitterly clinging to guns and religion. Specifically:

> You go into these small towns in Pennsylvania and, like a lot of small towns in the Midwest, the jobs have been gone now for twenty-five years and nothing's replaced them. And they fell through the Clinton administration, and the Bush administration, and each successive administration has said that somehow these communities are gonna regenerate and they have not. And it's not surprising then they get bitter, they cling to guns or religion or antipathy toward people who aren't like them or anti-immigrant sentiment or anti-trade sentiment as a way to explain their frustrations.

President Obama made his position even more clear after he took office when he reneged on his promise to take on China's currency manipulations.

In general, when running for office, Democrats pretend that they will do something about America's trade deficits. But, once elected, they do little to nothing. Michael Lind (2011) put it cleverly in an article he wrote for *The American Prospect*, a liberal magazine: "[T]rade divides the Democrats more than any other issue. The division is peculiar: It splits Democratic presidents into two people, the candidate and the elected official."

Furthermore, it's not only Democratic *presidents* who are duplicitous. From 2008 through 2012, members of the Democratic majority parties in the House and Senate almost all voted in favor of ending China's currency manipulations without actually passing anything. In 2010, the House passed an anti-currency-manipulation bill, but the Democrat leadership in the Senate tabled it. In 2012, the Senate passed a weak anti-currency-manipulation bill, knowing that the Republican leadership of the House would table it.

Why the duplicity? According to Bob Dreyfus (2010), writing in *The Nation*, there are deep divisions within the progressive community. On the one side, manufacturing workers' unions want to see tough action against China's trade manipulations, but on the other side, many progressives are pleased that China's communist government has been able to pull so many poor people out of poverty. He cites one progressive who accuses those who want to deal with China's unbalanced trade policy as being "yellow peril" racists.

When taking action, Obama has usually moved to switch the United States to state-capitalism (also called "crony capitalism" or "fascism") in an attempt to out-mercantilist the mercantilists. He picks future winners which he finances, subsidizes and promotes including green companies, the unionized automobile manufacturing companies, and the intersection between the two, the electric car.

The President's 2010 Trade Policy Agenda (Kirk 2010) announced President Obama's goal to increase U.S. exports. He created a new bureaucracy called the Export Promotion Cabinet to fund export promotion programs, tools for small- and medium-sized businesses, reduction in barriers to trade, and open new markets. According to the agenda, government officials were to select which industries should be promoted:

> Key cabinet agency officials including the United States Trade Representative and the Secretary of Commerce, along with the Council of Economic Advisers, the National Economic Council, and the National Security Council carefully analyzed growth trends in the world economy and policies the Administration could pursue to help improve U.S. export performance over the 2009–2014 period. (p. 1)

Although we doubt that the government is likely to be effective at picking winners, our principal concern with this agenda is that it offers little substance concerning balancing trade. Unfortunately, the only answer offered concerning how we were going to increase our exports to the world's fastest growing market, China, was that we will talk about it with them.

The agenda states: "Countries with large trade surpluses should increase their domestic consumption and imports as part of a more balanced growth strategy" (p. 3). But, with China growing rapidly while its western opponents' economies were stagnant, why would it change its policy without being forced to do so?

The agenda announced that President Obama had set a goal "of doubling U.S. exports in the next five years" to create two million jobs (p. 1). Half way through the goal, in September 2012, it was already clear that the plan was failing. U.S. exports had only risen by 25 percent, and imports had risen even faster. The number of manufacturing jobs had gone up by 481,000 to 11,958,000, but that was still 601,000 less than the number of manufacturing jobs when Obama took office.

So, why did Obama's plan fail? The answer is simple: He didn't do anything about mercantilism. He created a new bureaucracy called the Export Promotion Cabinet, which joined hundreds of federal agencies designed to do good but which ended up doing nothing. Just how was the United States going to increase its exports with the world's fastest growing markets excluding so many of its goods?

Alan Tonelson (2010) of the American Economic Alert paired a revealing set of quotes of Secretary of Commerce Gary Locke in a May 10, 2010, blog posting ("Obama Administration's China Trade Brain-Locke"):

- "We believe increasing our exports to China—not limiting our imports from China—is the best way to address the trade deficit."—Secretary of Commerce Gary Locke, May 4, 2010.
- The United States is concerned "about China's increasing use of industrial policies that may restrict market access and discriminate against foreign goods and services"—Secretary of Commerce Gary Locke, May 4, 2010.

On November 21, 2011, U.S. Secretary of Commerce John Bryson told reporters at the U.S.–China Joint Commission on Commerce and Trade (JCCT) that China planned to expand its subsidies in what it considered to be the "strategic sectors" of its economy (Buckley 2011). Previously, China had said that these sectors include vehicles, alternative energy, biotechnology, and advanced equipment manufacturing. Under WTO rules, developing countries are allowed to declare certain sectors of their economy to be "strategic sectors" and are allowed to charge high tariffs (about 25 percent) on imports into these sectors. China's definition of "strategic sectors" keeps expanding.

As a result of both the U.S. government and the Chinese government financing solar producers, there was a massive glut of solar panels worldwide. The Obama administration desperately tried to protect its investment as one after another U.S. solar panel producers started to go bankrupt by imposing tariffs of 31 to 250 percent on Chinese solar companies, and applying the tariffs retroactively (ninety days).

Whether or not the Obama administration's investment choices were well placed, the failure of the subsidies in their avowed goal of gaining U.S. market position in green energy reflected the great difficulties associated with any effort to out-mercantilist and out-industrial policy the mercantilists and state capitalists. In fact, according to a December 3, 2012, article in *Forbes* ("First Solar, Sun Power Ink Major Deals in China"), some of the American companies that are surviving appear to be moving production of new solar technologies to China.

Similarly, the Obama Administration's investment in electric cars helped boost the creation of the electric car technologies that were soon transferred to China, due to China's 25 percent tariff on American vehicles. On September 16, 2011, the Wall Street Journal reported ("Road Gets Bumpy for GM in China") that GM was trying to access the Chinese electric-car market without giving up its state-of-the-art electric-car technology. Here's a selection:

> GM would like to bring its Volt electric car into China. But Chief Executive Dan Akerson said he refuses to share electric-car technology in exchange for hefty consumer rebates from the Chinese government that would juice sales of the vehicle.

Just one week later, on September 22, the *New York Times* reported ("GM to develop electric cars with China") that GM had caved to the Chinese government demand:

> HONG KONG: General Motors said Tuesday that it would develop electric cars in China through a joint venture with a Chinese automaker [SAIC], and would transfer battery and other electric car technology to the venture.

President Obama thought that he could beat China at its own game of subsidy and industrial policy. He failed. The United States need not pick winners and losers to stop mercantilism. All it need do is require balanced trade. We should take a page from Keynes and the 1930s British Empire which ended U.S. mercantilism by resisting it. Is it truly liberal, progressive, or Democratic to sell out the economic foundations of the U.S. working class through ineffective policies that fail to balance trade, and through massive subsidies to businesses that fail to produce jobs?

THE REPUBLICAN FREE TRADE POSITION

Almost all Republican politicians support free trade; only a handful of Republicans object when free trade agreements are voted on in Congress. Within the Republican establishment, there is little interest in pursuing policies that might upset large donors in the multinational business establishment. The trade policy staffer for one Republican member of Congress told one of us that although he personally thought a policy to robustly balance trade was important, he couldn't advise his boss to support it because it would end his boss's political career.

Many Republican politicians argue that free trade is an important way to support the global progress of capitalism. During the Republican presidential primary campaign George W. Bush (1999) articulated his reasons for supporting open trade with China as follows:

> It's in our best interests to sell to the Chinese, and to make sure that the entrepreneurial class in China flourishes. If we make China an enemy, they'll end up being an enemy. If we trade with China, and trade with the entrepreneurial class, and give people a taste of freedom, I think you'll be amazed at how soon democracy will come.

Bush's pursuit of trade with China led less to opening of China's markets to American firms than to an aggressive takeover of American markets by Chinese-made goods. As discussed elsewhere, the trade deficit with China ballooned.

Pursuing free trade, according to Bush, was a way to promote the interests of China's entrepreneurs, a group which he hoped would then push for democratization. Unfortunately, Bush's vision of a rapidly democratizing China has been slow to materialize. Instead, the Chinese Communist Party (CCP) has successfully integrated the Chinese entrepreneurial class into a system of state capitalism.

Political scientist Jie Chen (2013) conducted a series of surveys in urban China to assess the attitudes of the Chinese entrepreneurial and middle classes. His findings throw cold water on Bush's hopes. Chen found that, compared to other classes in China, the Chinese middle class "tends to be more supportive of the current Party-state but less supportive of democratic values and institutions." In another study (Chen and Dickson 2010, 150), he found that many members of the entrepreneurial class are members of the CCP, particularly those who control larger companies. As a whole, China's capitalists "are not eager to support and participate in fundamental political change toward a democratic system characterized by multi-party competition and political liberties."

Bush also appeared to assume that increasing trade volumes will necessarily translate into peace. One important reason for the failure of the American political class to do anything about trade is the illusion that accepting trade on ruinous terms serves a broader national interest in peace. This view has shaky empirical foundations. Katherine Barbieri (2002) summed up the problems with the empirical evidence that trade promotes peace in her book *The Liberal Illusion* as follows:

> When taken as a whole, what should be obvious from the trade-conflict literature is the absence of firm evidence that trade promotes peace. If such evidence existed, I would expect this relationship to remain robust across studies. (p. 77)

Instead, Barbieri found that some authors adduce evidence that trade promotes peace while others find that it increases the incidence of war. The interaction of multiple complex factors condition the extent to which peace follows from high levels of trade, factors which the literature has not yet fully disentangled. In the years since Barbieri's book was published, scholars have continued to reach contradictory results, with some studies finding evidence that trade leads to conflict, and others finding that trade diminishes conflict. This contradictory empirical literature is hardly a sufficient basis for unilateral and imbalanced free trade, given the range of problems caused by trade deficits.

In one respect, Bush's arguments are on target. We believe it does not make sense to target trade with China in particular when the United States aims to balance trade overall. Instead, the United States should adopt policies which apply the same criteria to all countries with which it has large trade deficits. China would be significantly affected by such policies because the trade deficit with China is so large, but it should not be the only country affected.

Many Republicans and conservatives oppose any action aimed at balancing trade. Terry Miller (2010), writing on the Heritage Foundation's website ("Obama's Mercantilist Approach to Trade"), objected, as we do, to the haughty idea that government bureaucrats should pick which industries will be promoted. But he goes much further than that. He objects, even, to the goal of balancing trade. He calls Obama a "mercantilist," making two fundamental mistakes: (1) he mistakes talk for action, and (2) he equates self-defense with mercantilism. Here is the passage in which he equates self-defense against mercantilism with mercantilism:

> [Obama's] 2010 Trade Agenda is a recipe for economic failure and stagnation. Much of the focus is on enforcing rules to restrict other countries' access to the U.S. market. It's a beggar-thy-neighbor approach in which we would sell more to other countries while restricting their ability to sell to us. Such a model is unsustainable internationally: not every country can run a trade surplus.

Miller was ignoring the fact that the United States had a huge trade *deficit*. We were the *victim* of beggar-thy-neighbor economic attacks, not the perpetrator. Partly as a result of implementing Heritage Foundation recommendations, President Bush presided over a decline in American median incomes from 2001–2008, with the Asian mercantilists getting millions of middle-class manufacturing jobs. The result was that, by 2008, the Republican Party had lost the House, the Senate, and the presidency.

Republican politicians and intellectuals who object to or identify problems with free trade ideology are relegated to the political sidelines far too often. Nonetheless, a number of Republican politicians and conservative intellectuals have taken better positions on trade. For example, one of the Heritage Foundation's founders, Paul Weyrich, took a very different position on trade from the Heritage Foundation in his posthumous 2009 book *The Next Conservatism*, which he wrote with William S. Lind of the Free Congress Foundation. They argued:

> If economic efficiency means, for example, that America should send all its manufacturing jobs overseas, as free trade seems to demand, the next conservatism should not say, "Oh, well, I guess we have to go along with it." Better we toss our *sabots* into free trade's grinding gears. Economic security requires that people be able to get good-paying jobs, which means manufacturing jobs. (p. 112)

We agree. But Weyrich and Lind were likely wrong about the culprit. Economic efficiency occurs when trade is balanced. We trade a basket of goods that we produce with relative efficiency to our trading partners in return for a basket of goods that they produce with relative efficiency. Both countries gain jobs in efficient industries while losing jobs in inefficient industries. In consequence both we and our trading partners are better off as a result of trade.

On the other hand, Weyrich and Lind were clearly correct that our unilateral free trade policy was destroying one of America's great accomplishments. They wrote:

> We must conserve and restore the well-paying jobs manufacturing offers to the blue-collar middle class, whose existence ought to be one of our proudest national achievements. (p. 113)

Weyrich and Lind were clearly on the right track. It is not conservative to elevate the totalitarian government of China to world-power status by giving it our industries. It is not conservative to tell manufacturing workers that the United States can't stop China from stealing their jobs. The *next conservatism* should substitute balanced trade for unilateral free trade in order to restore our prosperous blue-collar middle class while strengthening our economy.

Former Reagan speech writer Pat Buchanan (2011) also advocates a change in trade policy in order to preserve the American middle class. In a Labor Day 2011 commentary ("How Capital Crushed Labor"), he gives a history of the U.S. trade deficits. At first we built our industries behind tariff walls, running continuous trade surpluses that benefited our economy and financed our government. Then we went globalist:

> By 1976. . . . The new idea was to replicate America on a global scale, to throw open the borders of all nations as the borders of the fifty states were open, to abolish all tariffs and trade barriers, and to welcome the free flow of goods and people across all frontiers, thereby creating the One World that statesmen such as Woodrow Wilson and Wendell Willkie had envisioned. . . .
>
> Already established in the U.S. market, corporate America could risk sharing that market if, in return, it could shift its own production out of the United States to countries where the wages were low and regulations were light.

Buchanan had an important part of the story, but not the whole story. The rest of the story was that "U.S." came to stand for "Uncle Sucker." We let our trading partners practice mercantilism to gain market share in their competition with our industries, beginning with Germany and Japan, but soon joined by many other countries.

We don't have to turn our backs on trade, and we don't have to let our trading partners run trade surpluses with us. There is a third alternative which, so far, only two Republican politicians of note have advocated—balanced trade.

The *Los Angeles Times* reported that Governor Palin met with Donald Trump during a May 31, 2011, visit to New York ("Donald Trump and Sarah Palin have a Pizza Summit in New York") when she was considering running for the 2012 Republican nomination for president. In her remarks, she told reporters that she advocates balanced trade arrangements:

> What do we have in common? Our love for this country, a desire to see our economy put back on the right track. . . . To have a balanced trade arrangement with other countries across this world so Americans can have our jobs, our industries, our manufacturing again. And exploiting responsibly our natural resources. We can do that again if we make good decisions.

True conservatism never changes. It is the system of thought that tells us that the past has much to teach us about the present. It attempts to preserve the best from the past, while keeping trust with the future. Conservatism teaches that ideology doesn't provide all of the answers. Often it must engage in a careful analysis of the costs and benefits of a policy action, including the unintended consequences. The very antithesis of conservative policy is a policy of unilateral free trade that cashiers the legacy of past generations and steers future generations toward poverty in order to increase current consumption and pursue an idealized world that doesn't exist.

WHY ARE BOTH PARTIES WEAK ON TRADE?

When Democrats campaign on trade, the Democratic narrative is that U.S. trade deficits are caused by Republicans who take the side of big business against the American worker. Whenever possible, it claims that Republicans are tied to outsourcing businesses. Here are some examples taken from 2010 campaigns, as reported on September 18, 2010, by the Associated Press (Espo 2010):

- "New York Democratic Rep. Tim Bishop unleashed a television ad christening [businessman Randy Altschuler] an 'outsourcing pioneer' who sent jobs overseas while millions of Americans struggle . . . an announcer adds that Altschuler 'made millions outsourcing jobs.'"
- "In California, where unemployment stood at 12.3 percent in July, Sen. Barbara Boxer recently began running a commercial that says Republican candidate Carly Fiorina laid off 30,000 workers while she was CEO of computer giant Hewlett-Packard."
- "In other cases, including races in Wisconsin, Illinois, Nevada, Virginia and elsewhere, Democrats have seized on a no-tax-increase pledge signed by Republican incumbents or candidates as evidence they want to protect breaks for companies that export jobs."

The Republican establishment's counter narrative is that the Democrats support protectionism while Republicans support free trade. Unfortunately, this rhetoric ignores the fact that American trade with mercantilist countries is not free. Moreover, the American people are not buying it.

Public opinion on trade has shifted decisively against the unilateral free trade position. An October 2007 Wall Street Journal/NBC News poll (Hart/Newhouse 2007) found that 59 percent of *Republicans* agreed with the statement that: "Foreign trade has been bad for the U.S. economy, because imports from abroad have reduced demand for American-made goods, cost jobs here at home, and produced potentially unsafe products."

Similarly, a poll conducted in April 2010 for the Alliance for American Manufacturing (Mellman and Ayres 2010) found that 71 percent of the American people would: "Impose tariffs on products from China unless it stops cheating on its trade commitments with the United States."

A solid majority of the American people favor steps that would transform U.S. trade policy. A December 2010 national poll (Allstate/National Journal 2010) contained an extensive battery of questions on trade and U.S. manufacturing. The poll revealed strong public majorities against free trade. For example, 68 percent of respondents supported a policy requiring that "a certain percentage of every high-end manufactured product, such as automobiles, heavy machinery, and transportation equipment, sold in the United States be produced or assembled within the United States, even if that means higher prices for their products." Similarly, only 21 percent of respondents favored the pursuit of more free trade agreements, as opposed to 73 percent who favored either tariffs or subsidies to strengthen America's competitive position.

In an attempt to change the narrative, Republican presidential candidate Romney claimed that he would get much tougher on China than Obama if elected, but Romney made only limited inroads with blue collar workers, partly because of Obama's negative campaign attacks which branded Romney as a businessman who had engaged in outsourcing. With no candidate representing their interests turnout declined in 2012 among blue collar workers (Trende 2012).

If they want to keep their narrative that they are looking out for American workers, Democrats should start walking the walk, not just talking the talk. If Republicans wish to change that narrative, they need to abandon the Republican establishment's unilateral free trade policy. The public is losing faith in both parties (Alliance for American Manufacturing 2014), with none evaluated positively by a majority in 2014 polling. If neither party is willing to act, America may need a third party that advocates balanced trade. Ross Perot had it right.

6

The Failure of the Federal Reserve

Singapore-based economist Richard Duncan (2005) predicted something very much like the Great Recession of 2008. Duncan understood that the trade-deficit countries, especially the United States, would not be able to continue purchasing more and more imports without the income that would come from selling exports. Countries can only borrow so much from abroad to buy imports until they experience financial crises.

But when the Great Recession hit in October 2008, American economic leaders pretended that the U.S. economy could be fixed without balancing trade, simply by shoveling debt from the public sector to the private sector and by engaging in fiscal and monetary stimuli. It didn't work well. The reason? The emerging markets continued their mercantilist buying of foreign currency reserves in order to manipulate exchange rates, as shown in figure 6.1. As a result, they grew out of the recession in 2009, while the advanced economies, their victims, faltered, as shown in figure 6.2.

Since 1996, the Federal Reserve had been failing to deal with the rise of mercantilism. In fact, under Bernanke's predecessor Alan Greenspan, the Federal Reserve actually made our trade deficits much worse and set the stage for both the 1998–2000 stock market bubble and the 1998 to 2006 house price bubble by responding in exactly the wrong way.

Greenspan was chairman of the Federal Reserve from August 1987 to February 2006. During that period he did a good job of maintaining a steady money supply. He appeared to follow the monetarist prescription that the Federal Reserve should increase the money supply at a slightly faster rate than the economy is growing in order to maintain economic stability.

But Greenspan did nothing to stop increased foreign central bank dollar purchases, which accelerated throughout the late 1990s and 2000s, even though he could have counteracted them by buying the same amount of foreign currency

Figure 6.1. Currency Manipulations Sept. 2009–Sept. 2010

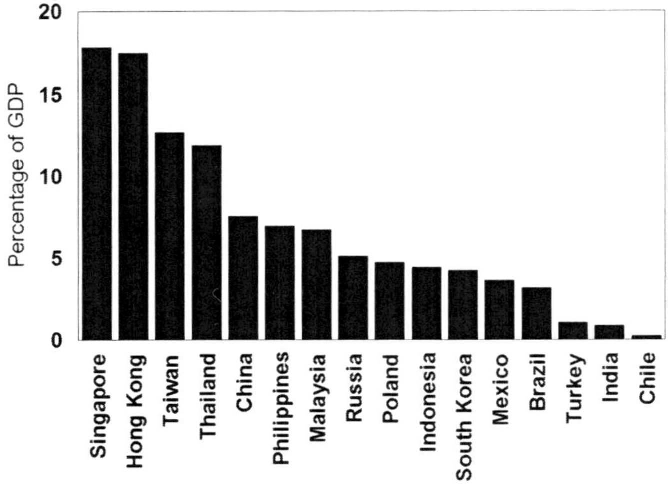

Reserve accumulations as a percentage of their GDPs by emerging market countries from September 2009 to September 2010. Source: Federal Reserve data for Chairman Bernanke's speech in Frankfurt Germany on November 19, 2010.

Figure 6.2. Real GDP of Emerging and Advanced Countries

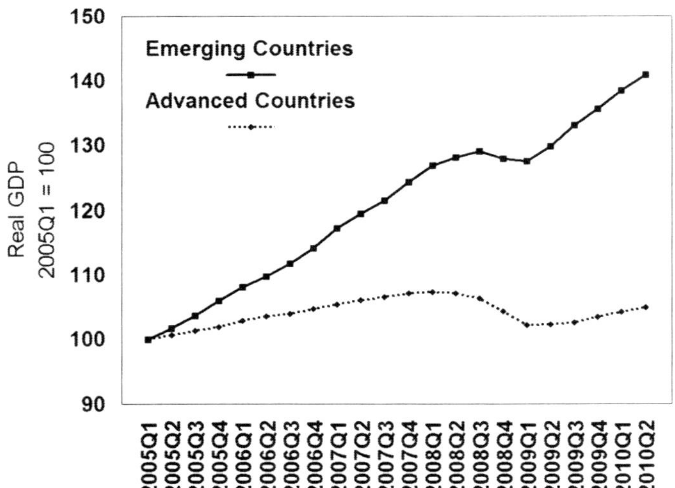

Output by emerging market countries and advanced countries. Source: Federal Reserve data for Chairman Bernanke's speech in Frankfurt Germany on November 19, 2010.

reserves, as the Federal Reserve is allowed to do without approval from the U.S. Treasury. Instead, he sat by while his fellow central banks bought U.S. dollar reserves so that their manufacturers would gain market share in their competition with U.S. manufacturers.

In 1997 Greenspan made his worst mistake. He let the currencies of the Asian Tigers, including South Korea, collapse without offering their central banks currency swaps that they could have used to stabilize their currencies. Especially galling was his failure to help South Korea. Due to the falling *won* versus the dollar, many South Korean businesses that had borrowed money in dollar-denominated loans, couldn't make their loan payments, so they and the banks that had loaned them the money were facing bankruptcy. In his memoirs, Greenspan (2007, 188–189) noted that the Federal Reserve had been in touch with the South Korean central bank, but had not offered it a single loan. He wrote:

> When Charlie Siegman, one of our top international economists phoned a Korean central banker on Thanksgiving and asked, "Why don't you release more of your reserves?" the banker answered, "We don't have any." What they'd published as reserves were already spoken for.

The collapse demonstrated the unwillingness of the Federal Reserve to help countries that were facing the international equivalent of a bank run. After the collapse, many Asian Tigers, including South Korea, decided to build up their dollar reserves in order to stabilize their currencies should future crises arrive. They soon found that by buying dollar reserves they could keep their currencies' exchange rates low and gain market share for their producers.

In short, the Asian Tigers were pushed by Greenspan into a successful mercantilist strategy as a result of their currency collapses. They were soon building up dollar reserves far in excess of what they might ever need. Meanwhile, due to the rising dollar, U.S. trade deficits exploded as U.S. producers lost market share. And, still, Greenspan failed to buy reciprocal amounts of foreign currencies.

Instead, Greenspan responded to the currency collapses of the Asian Tigers by increasing the American money supply so that increased American consumer spending would help stabilize the world economy through an expanded U.S. trade deficit. It worked. But at a cost. The United States lost millions of manufacturing jobs and experienced a destructive stock bubble followed by an even more destructive house price bubble.

At the end of January 2006, Ben Bernanke replaced Greenspan as the head of the Federal Reserve. In order to get the position, he had to persuade the Senate that he would do something about Asian mercantilism. In a lecture entitled *The Global Saving Glut and the U.S. Current Account Deficit*, Bernanke (2005) explained that a "global savings glut" was largely responsible for the U.S. trade deficit and that one of the important causes of that glut was the buildup of dollar reserves by governments pursuing export-led growth strategies. Specifically, Bernanke said:

> In practice, these countries increased reserves through the expedient of issuing debt to their citizens, thereby mobilizing domestic saving, and then using the proceeds to buy U.S. Treasury securities and other assets. Effectively, governments have acted as financial intermediaries, channeling domestic saving away from local uses and into international capital markets.

The idea of a "global savings glut" was a bit deceptive. The countries sending their savings to the United States were deliberately preventing those savings from being available to borrowers in their own countries. Absent government mobilization of savings to channel them into U.S. Treasury securities, those savings would likely have remained at home. Also, the idea that these countries were following export-led growth strategies ignored the fact that they were keeping out imports at the same time. They were practicing mercantilism, pure and simple.

In a long speech devoted to the growing income inequality problem within the United States, Bernanke (2007) acknowledged that a loss of jobs in import-competing industries was indeed occurring, but argued that such jobs would be replaced by jobs in exporting industries. Specifically:

> International trade, another aspect of globalization, may also have differential effects on the economic well-being of U.S. workers, even as it tends to raise real wages and incomes on average. For example, some empirical research suggests that, in the 1980s and 1990s, increased international trade reduced the profitability and hence the demand for labor in a number of industries that employed relatively low skilled workers (Borjas, Freeman, and Katz, 1997; Sachs and Shatz, 1994). Of course trade has increased the *potential* [italics ours] markets for other domestic industries, leading to higher demand and thus higher real wages for workers in those industries.

Although this argument sounded plausible, it had a $760 billion hole in it at the time. The word "potential" is key to understanding his fallacy. The jobs in exporting industries were only "potential" jobs, not actual jobs. *Because of the trade deficits, these jobs did not exist.*

In October 2008, Bernanke showed that he had learned at least one thing from Greenspan's 1997 mistake. When the dollar spiked upward in foreign exchange markets due to a sudden international liquidity crunch following the Lehman Brothers collapse, he offered currency swaps to friendly central banks so that they could borrow dollars and use them to strengthen their own currencies or help their own businesses pay dollar-denominated loans. It was Bernanke's finest hour.

Bernanke's currency swaps of October 2008 demonstrated the responsibility of the central bank that manages a currency which is used in international trade. As trade grows, it needs to make increasing amounts of its currency available abroad to finance international transactions. There are two ways that enough dollars can build up abroad:

1. *One Sided Flows.* One way occurs when a foreign central bank builds up its dollar reserves without the Federal Reserve building up reserves in that foreign

currency. This method causes the dollar to strengthen versus the foreign currency in foreign exchange markets and causes the foreign currency to weaken versus the dollar in foreign exchange markets.

2. *Two Sided Flows.* The other way occurs when two central banks swap each others currencies. This method does not cause any change in the relative value of the two currencies. If foreign central banks do not cooperate with the Federal Reserve, then the Federal Reserve can simply buy the same value of their currency reserves that they buy of our reserves.

It is worth emphasizing that two-sided flows provide a solution to the "Triffin paradox." Some economists, following Robert Triffin (1960), assume that trade deficits are inevitable in the country whose currency serves as the world's reserve currency. But there is nothing inevitable about them. Foreign dollar reserves can also be created through currency swaps without giving the United States trade deficits. Bernanke's currency swaps demonstrated this technique. Two-sided currency flows provide international liquidity without requiring trade imbalances.

Bernanke's management of the 2008 financial crisis has become known as QE1, for "Quantitative Easing 1." He single-handedly restored domestic and international liquidity by making loans freely available to private banks and currency swaps available to foreign central banks. In the process, he may have prevented a full-scale repeat of the Great Depression.

CENTRAL BANKING IN A GLOBALIZED WORLD

Nevertheless, the Great Recession continued. The Federal Reserve's usual monetary tools for growing the money supply in order to grow GDP were no longer working. The breakdown of international barriers to capital flows had created a situation in which central banks could not entirely control the domestic policy levers that they once controlled.

Figure 6.3 shows the annual growth rates of nominal GDP (GDP without adjusting for inflation) and M2 (the broader measure of money supply which includes cash, checking accounts, and money market accounts). In the 1960s, 1970s, and 1980s, growth in money supply appeared to cause corresponding growth in nominal GDP. When money supply grew by a certain percentage, GDP soon grew by about the same percentage. From 1960 through 1990, the correlation between M2 growth and GDP growth was 0.49. But beginning in the 1990s that apparent causation fell apart. The Federal Reserve's normal actions to grow money supply were having less and less effect upon nominal GDP growth. From 1990 through 2012, the correlation was actually negative, -0.37.

Studies by Martin Feldstein explain why the Federal Reserve had been losing control. Once, when Feldstein was attending a conference of international economists, he realized that two branches of economists had completely different theories

Figure 6.3. GDP and Money Supply

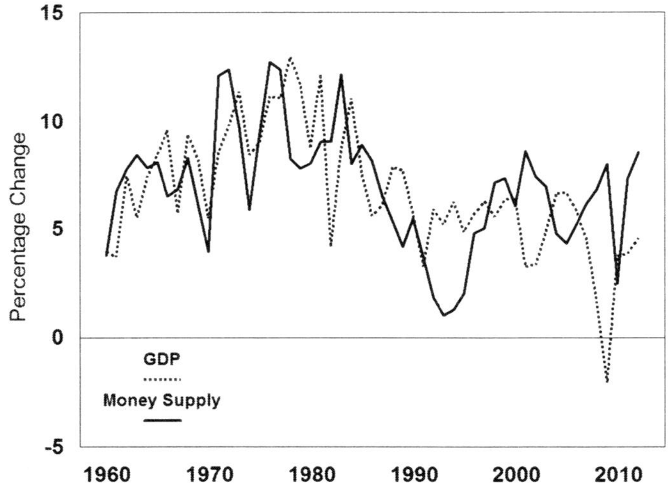

The close relationship between nominal GDP and money supply (M2) broke down in the 1990s. Source: M2 from the Federal Reserve, GDP from the BEA.

regarding how interest rates are determined. The branch that studied public policy assumed that the Federal Reserve could control the U.S. interest rate. The branch that studied international economics assumed that the international market for capital determined the U.S. interest rate. Here's how Feldstein (2005, 1–2) described this experience in a speech:

> As an outsider to the fraternity of international economics specialists, I was surprised that all of the discussion at that meeting assumed that the textbook view of complete capital market integration was a correct description of the real world. My sense of surprise reflected the fact that the implications of such complete global capital market integration contradicted my view. . . . [T]he integrated global capital market view also implied that a large fiscal deficit would not reduce domestic investment or raise the domestic interest rate.

He wondered who was right. Were international capital markets integrated, meaning that macroeconomic policies would not affect U.S. interest rates, or were they segmented, meaning that macroeconomic policies would affect interest rates?

The first of Feldstein's studies of the subject (Horoika and Feldstein 1980) found that markets were basically segmented during the period from 1960 through 1974 for the sixteen OECD countries. However, as Feldstein reported in that 2005 speech, by the decade ending in 2002, capital market segmentation had practically disappeared. As a consequence, central banks were losing control over their economies.

Feldstein was not blind to the fact that many Asian Central Banks, especially the People's Bank of China, were marshalling their savings and investing them in U.S. assets, not responding to market forces, and that such flows make it more difficult for the Federal Reserve to fight inflation through monetary policy because any given rise in U.S. short-term interest rates would be less contractionary. They also make it difficult for the Federal Reserve to fight a recession because long-term interest rates would not fall in response to a reduction in short-term interest rates.

Feldstein was aware that the growing savings inflows were coming from countries that he identified as America's "Asian trading partners" (p. 9). Permitting these inflows was causing the Federal Reserve to lose its control over consumption, investment, inflation, and unemployment within the U.S. economy.

In March 2009, Bernanke finally began addressing the U.S. trade deficits. He began a speech (Bernanke 2009) at the Council on Foreign Relations by pointing out that global imbalances lay at the heart of America's financial crisis. Only the first part of Bernanke's speech was about imbalanced trade. He began:

> The world is suffering through the worst financial crisis since the 1930s, a crisis that has precipitated a sharp downturn in the global economy. Its fundamental causes remain in dispute. In my view, however, it is impossible to understand this crisis without reference to the global imbalances in trade and capital flows that began in the latter half of the 1990s. . . .
>
> The global imbalances were the joint responsibility of the United States and our trading partners, and although the topic was a perennial one at international conferences, we collectively did not do enough to reduce those imbalances.

In May of 2010, Bernanke finally began to take action, but it was the wrong action. Instead of calling upon the president and Congress to require balanced trade, instead of buying the currency reserves of the very countries that were buying dollars in order to grow or maintain their trade surpluses with the United States, he increased the money supply by buying long-term U.S. government bonds, a strategy known as QE2 (the second "Quantitative Easing"). During the twelve months ending in May 2011, the Federal Reserve grew M1 (the narrow measure of money supply which includes cash and checking accounts) at a 13.4 percent rate.

QE2 was designed to reduce American private savings and also to cause private American and foreign savings to leave the United States and go elsewhere. Bernanke's goal was to increase inflation from its current 1 percent while keeping short-term U.S. interest rates close to 0 percent, producing an "inflation tax" upon private American and foreign savers.

German Finance Minister Wolfgang Schäuble criticized Bernanke's policy as being a form of exchange rate manipulation. Here is a selection from his November interview with *Der Spiegel* (2010):

> *SPIEGEL:* The U.S. wants to depress the value of the dollar in this way, so that it can sell its products abroad more easily. In light of the ailing U.S. economy, isn't that a completely reasonable strategy?

> *SCHÄUBLE:* No. The Fed's decisions bring more uncertainty to the global economy. They make it more difficult to achieve a reasonable balance between industrialized and emerging economies, and they undermine the U.S.'s credibility when it comes to fiscal policy. It's inconsistent for the Americans to accuse the Chinese of manipulating exchange rates and then to artificially depress the dollar exchange rate by printing money.

Bernanke hoped that reducing private American savings would increase American consumption and that sending private savings abroad would cause the exchange rate of the dollar to decline which would improve America's trade balance. Indeed, the short-term result of QE2 was beneficial. Consumption increased and private savings fled the country for better interest rates abroad. The dollar immediately weakened versus most foreign currencies, which made American products more competitive in the United States and world markets.

But those effects were short-lived; Bernanke soon had to take his foot off the pedal. As shown in figure 6.4, inflation began to rise in November 2010, reaching 3.6 percent for the twelve months ending in May 2011, even though Bernanke (2010) had told his fellow central bankers in November 2010 that the Federal Reserve's Open Market Committee (FOMC) was targeting an inflation rate no higher than 2 percent.

Figure 6.4. Inflation Rate during QE2

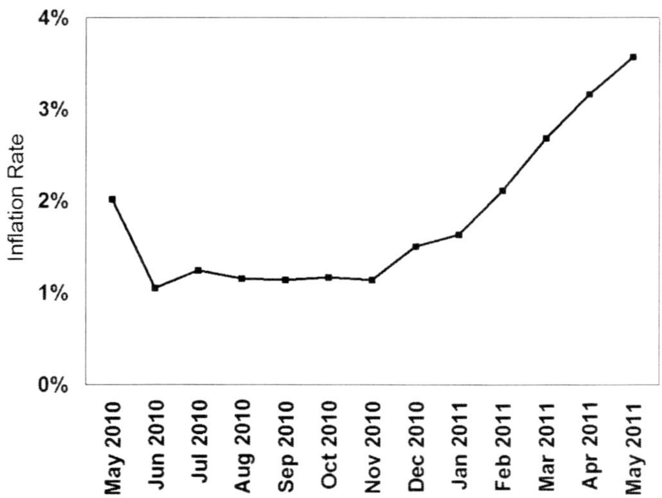

Over the course of QE2 (the second quantitative easing by the Federal Reserve), the inflation rate, as measured by the Consumer Price Index, grew from 1.1 percent for the twelve months ending in June 2010 to 3.6 percent for the twelve months ending in May 2011, which exceeded the Federal Reserve's 2 percent inflation target. Source: inflationdata.com.

Furthermore, the effect of QE2 upon the dollar depended upon foreign central banks. The People's Bank of China simply tightened its money supply to head off inflation and bought enough dollars to continue growing its trade surpluses with the United States. As shown in figure 6.5, the U.S. merchandise trade balance fell from a negative $236 billion for the twelve months ending in May 2010 to a negative $287 billion for the twelve months ending in May 2011.

On the other hand, QE2 did drive up the price of the currencies of several "innocent bystander" countries giving them trade deficits. By 2013, some of these countries were experiencing financial difficulties. According to an OECD (2013, 13) report:

> Reinforced by concerns about growth slowdowns and the sustainability of high external [trade] deficits and political tensions in some economies, large portfolio investment outflows contributed to tighter liquidity conditions, sharp declines in bond and stock prices, and sizable currency depreciations. This was especially marked in Brazil, India, Indonesia, South Africa, and Turkey, all countries with large external financing needs.

The big loser as these countries' economies readjust will be the United States. In 2012, the United States had about a twelve billion dollars trade surplus with these five countries. In 2014, due to their financial problems and lower exchange rates, this small surplus can be expected to turn into a deficit.

Figure 6.5. Trade Balance with China during QE2

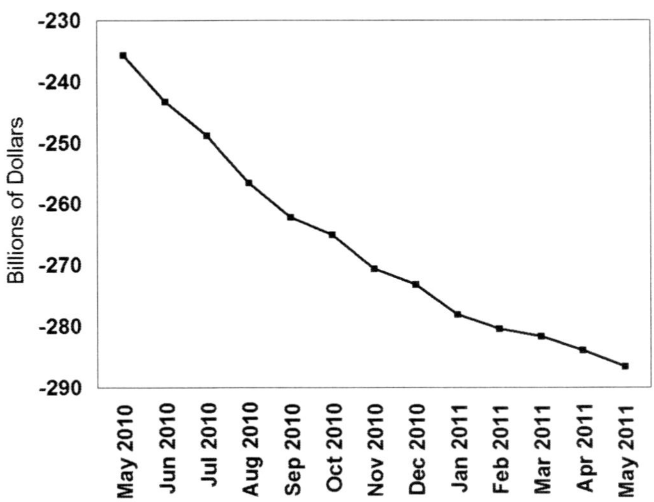

Over the course of QE2 (the second quantitative easing by the Federal Reserve), the U.S. merchandise trade balance with China fell from a negative $236 billion for the twelve months ending in May 2010 to a negative $287 for the twelve months ending in May 2011. Source: Census Bureau.

COULD THE FEDERAL RESERVE BALANCE TRADE?

Since 1962, the Federal Reserve has had the power to buy foreign currencies under its own account without being subject to any control by the U.S. Treasury. In 2008, Bernanke took advantage of that power when he engaged in currency swaps with friendly central banks during the 2008 financial crisis, but he ignored that power during QE2.

As we pointed out in 2008, a central bank can neutralize a fellow central bank's reserve purchases by buying the exact same amount of that central bank's reserves. We wrote: "Whenever the Federal Reserve responds in kind with reciprocal actions to the monetary mercantilist policies of foreign central banks, the effects would be exactly the same as if each central bank were minding its own economy" (Richman, Richman, and Richman 2008, 160).

In a Peterson Institute for International Economics Policy Brief, C. Fred Bergsten and Joseph E. Gagnon (2012) essentially recommended such purchases which they called CCI ("Countervailing Currency Intervention"). They proposed that the United States combat currency manipulations by China, Denmark, Hong Kong, South Korea, Malaysia, Singapore, Switzerland, and Taiwan, which they saw as the chief unjustified currency manipulators of that time.

Greenspan and Bernanke could have tried to counteract the capital inflows forced into the United States by the mercantilist central banks. They could have advocated that Congress and/or the president impose a trade balancing tariff. But, instead, they presided over the Federal Reserve while the United States lost market share in one industry after another, experienced a house price bubble fed by foreign loans, eventually experienced falling median incomes, and eventually experienced high unemployment.

CONCLUSION

In a world in which capital markets are integrated, central banks lose control over their capital markets. The only effective actions that are left to them are actions which affect the outflow and inflow of capital. Greenspan's action in 1997 made the U.S. trade deficits worse. The action that Bernanke took in 2011 never made a dent in the growing U.S. trade deficit with China, but hurt "innocent bystanders" which buy more from the United States when the United States buys more from them.

If U.S. trade were kept balanced through an effective trade balancing regime, the United States would no longer get a net inflow of foreign capital. Its capital market would, in effect, be segmented from that of the rest of the world. At that point, the Federal Reserve's normal monetary policy tools for growing the money supply would again be effective.

III

THE SOLUTIONS

7

Reciprocity

Principles for Balanced Trade

If long-term trade deficits are a problem (chapters 1 through 3) which policymakers have failed to solve (chapters 4 through 6), then something new must be done. In this chapter we discuss the principles that will guide our search for a successful policy.

THE PRINCIPLE OF RECIPROCITY

In an op-ed, one of us laid out the principle that trade should be reciprocal (Richman 2003). Raymond began:

> Is there any way to balance our trade? Let's take a clue from the fact that barter is always beneficial to both parties. Instead of "Free Trade" as the slogan, how about the slogan, "Free and Balanced Trade?" We could announce to countries with whom we have large chronic deficits that their exports to us in the future will be limited to, say, 110 percent of what we bought from them last year. If you want to trade with us, you'll have to buy from us. Let's barter!

This principle goes back at least as far as President Franklin D. Roosevelt, who articulated it after the British Commonwealth enacted the Imperial Preference System, in response to Smoot-Hawley. Roosevelt got authorization from Congress to negotiate reciprocal reductions in U.S. tariff rates in exchange for lower tariff rates on U.S. exports. Thus was born the 1934 Reciprocal Trade Agreements Act.

Roosevelt's great success was pulling Canada out of the Imperial Preference System in 1935, following the election of Liberal Party Prime Minister W. L. M. King. Ever since, the United States and Canada have shared low tariffs with little mercantilism, a model of how countries should trade.

Because there is the potential for mutually beneficial gains from trade, reciprocal negotiation has the potential to make all countries better off and increase global welfare. Unfortunately, just as Congress was shortsighted and overly focused on domestic concerns when it passed the Smoot-Hawley tariff, presidents proved to be shortsighted and insufficiently attentive to the economic welfare of the U.S. economy in their trade agreement negotiations.

Trade advantages became a convenient substitute for foreign aid in some cases. Furthermore, the political power of outsourcing and importing interests grew as the United States lowered trade barriers (Dür 2010; De Bievre and Eckhardt 2011). It is tautological that when countries are running large trade deficits, the gross revenue of exporters is dwarfed by the gross revenue of importers. Power appears to have followed the money.

In a campaign speech on September 29, 1932, in Sioux City, Iowa, President Roosevelt attempted to deflect concerns about how the reciprocal tariff negotiations would go:

> I have not the fear that possesses some timorous minds that we should get the worst of it in such reciprocal arrangements. I ask if you have no faith in our Yankee tradition of good old-fashioned trading? Do you believe that our early instincts for successful barter have degenerated or atrophied? I do not think so. I have confidence that the spirit of the stalwart traders still permeates our people, that the red blood of the men who sailed our Yankee clipper ships around the Horn and Cape of Good Hope in the China trade still courses in our veins.

But more than thirty years of unremitting trade deficits suggest that at in recent decades those "early instincts for barter" have indeed atrophied in favor of an acceptance of cheap consumption now in exchange for debt (and relative poverty) later.

A key problem is that tariff reciprocity, by itself, no longer works. Modern day mercantilists have *many* ways to keep trade out of balance, not just tariffs. Mercantilist governments typically manipulate trade balances through foreign asset purchases, export subsidies, and non-tariff barriers.

Any U.S. focus on tariff reciprocity misses the broader need for trade reciprocity and thus fails to provide the promised benefits. "Free trade," when radically imbalanced, is not desirable.

THE BENEFITS OF RECIPROCALLY BALANCED TRADE

If trade is balanced, many of the problems associated with trade deficits that we discussed in chapter 3 tend to disappear. For instance:

1. *Foreign debt, bubbles and reduced long-term consumption*. If trade is balanced, no net foreign debt accumulation occurs.

2. *Reduced GDP, median incomes, and employment.* If trade is balanced, jobs lost to imports are replaced by more productive jobs producing exports.
3. *Loss of manufacturing investment and innovation.* If trade is balanced, mercantilists cannot force manufacturers to build factories abroad.
4. *Loss of comparative advantage.* If trade is balanced, mercantilists cannot subsidize some of their industries without harming others.

However, balancing trade is difficult. For example, China's response to U.S. and European efforts to constrain its mercantilist policies is to threaten an escalating trade war in which some or all parties may lose. To win, the United States must transform the game by requiring reciprocity. The "game of chicken" (a long-studied model of conflict) offers insights into how the United States should proceed.

NOT CHICKENING OUT

Trade policy making is often modeled as a prisoner's dilemma between countries (e.g., Gowa and Mansfield 1993), and sometimes modeled as a coordination game (e.g., Snidal 1985). But typical treatments of trade negotiations make it too easy to ignore the strategic context of responding to mercantilism. What both coordination and prisoner's dilemma approaches make too easy to ignore is the potential for unequal equilibria in which both trading partners gain enough from trade to make semi-free trade preferable to protectionism, but one trading partner manipulates the terms of trade to capture much more of the gains from trade than the other. The long-studied model of conflict called "the game of chicken" provides a useful analogy.

In the game of chicken, two players must decide between aggressive and cooperative strategies. Mutual selection of cooperative strategies provides reasonably good payoffs for both. But each player is better off selecting an aggressive strategy when faced with an opponent who cooperates. In this situation, the cooperator suffers. The critical difference between "chicken" and the "prisoner's dilemma" is that the cooperator does not benefit from switching to an aggressive strategy when faced by an aggressive strategy. If both players select the aggressive strategy, both suffer enormous losses.

Figure 7.1 illustrates the payoffs for a simple version of the game of chicken. The two pure strategy Nash equilibria of the game are (Mercantilism, Free Trade) and (Free Trade, Mercantilism). If the United States chooses free trade and China chooses mercantilism, then the United States gets a payoff of one and China gets a payoff of six. But the United States has no incentive to switch to mercantilism itself (the payoff of this switch is zero). As discussed in chapter 5, Obama's efforts to out-mercantilist state-capitalist competitors failed.

In this game there are enough mutual advantages to trade that in equilibrium neither country wants to respond to mercantilism with mercantilism (the payoff of *one* is better than *zero*), but the benefits of trade are not distributed equally between the

Figure 7.1. Theoretical Payoffs for a Game of Chicken

The Game of Chicken		United States	
		Free Trade	Mercantilism
China	Free Trade	5 5	6 1
	Mercantilism	1 6	0 0

If the United States chooses free trade and China chooses mercantilism, then the United States gets a payoff of 1 and China gets a payoff of 6. If both countries choose free trade, then both countries get a payoff of 5.

trading partners. Mutual free trade (which would have the highest overall payoffs) is the cooperative strategy, but it is not a Nash Equilibrium. In other words, neither country benefits by changing its strategy if the other country's strategy remains unchanged.

For the last several decades, the United States has generally played a cooperative strategy on trade with China and other mercantilists. U.S. markets have been open to Chinese goods, and the United States supported Chinese membership in the World Trade Organization. American leaders selected free trade on the basis of the (false) hope that China would reciprocate by opening its markets to American firms. China, by contrast, has pursued an aggressive mercantilist strategy. If the payoffs for mercantilism are indeed similar to those from the game of chicken, then it is obvious that China has no incentive whatsoever to voluntarily shift from exploitation to cooperation (a payoff of six is better than a payoff of five).

As discussed in previous chapters, the fruits of mercantilist exploitation are evident. Many products developed in the United States are now produced almost entirely in China. The United States runs a large trade deficit with China on both high tech products and traditional industries like clothing and shoes. Meanwhile, in 2012 China purchased only about thirty-two cents worth of goods and services from the United States for every dollar of goods and services that Americans bought from China. In return for Chinese products, Americans go ever deeper into debt.

The game of chicken highlights the dilemma the United States faces if it attempts to adopt a more aggressive posture towards mercantilism by shifting to "mercantilism": both sides will be worse off. Although China's efforts to encourage Americans to steer clear of protectionism (Market Watch 2010a) because it would make both sides worse off may have some truth behind them (mercantilism versus mercantilism has the lowest payoffs for both), responding to mercantilism with free trade will continue driving the United States into increasing debt and continue the destruction of one American industry after another. And given the structure of the game, forcing China to cooperate is difficult.

U.S. actions aimed at balancing trade with China will likely meet resistance and counter-measures. Consider these examples:

1. *Chicken feet.* In February 2010 China announced that it was imposing tariffs of up to 105.4 percent on U.S. chicken exports (Kitchen 2010). One of the products in dispute was chicken feet. Because these are sold for ten times as much in China as in the United States, China accused U.S. chicken producers of dumping chicken feet below cost in the Chinese market. U.S. exports of chicken feet to China are a classic example of the gains trade makes available. A product that has little value in one economy is traded with another economy where consumers place more value on it. Both sides win. The chicken tariffs were announced after the United States placed anti-dumping tariffs on Chinese steel pipes and offended China by selling weapons to Taiwan, which China claims as its territory.
2. *Nylon and tires.* In April 2010 China announced that it would impose tariffs on American nylon products (Market Watch 2010b) after the Obama administration imposed tariffs on Chinese tires, even though the tire tariffs were authorized by China's agreement with the United States when it entered the World Trade Organization.

To get to the objective of free and balanced trade (mutual free trade), the U.S. government must adopt a game-changing strategy that provides mercantilists with incentives to cooperate in return for American cooperation. A cooperative pattern cannot be sustained unless the United States adopts strategies that provide all parties with incentives to sustain it. Sustaining cooperation requires the use of credible threats and promises that transform the incentives of the other player.

In terms of the game theory model, such a threat could have as its basis the mixed strategy equilibrium of the game. In the mixed strategy equilibrium, both players play free trade and mercantilism half of the time. This equilibrium offers payoffs of three to both players. Since the mixed strategy equilibrium has lower payoffs than mutual cooperation, mutual cooperation can be sustained by the threat to play the mixed strategy. The United States must pursue and enforce balanced trade in order to end imbalanced trade. It must stop chickening out. In practical terms, what should such a strategy be and accomplish?

1. *It should be effective.* A strategy that doesn't balance trade fails to accomplish the primary objective. A strategy that depends upon unrealistic assumptions about the actions of other nations will not accomplish the objective of balancing trade.
2. *It should be efficient.* The cost of implementation should be low, and the risks of undesirable or unanticipated side effects should be low or manageable. It should lead to a free trade–free trade outcome not a mercantilism–mercantilism outcome.
3. *It should be as consistent as possible with international law.* Strategies that violate international law risk wrecking good aspects of the international trading system along with problematic ones. They would also be much more difficult and costly to implement and sustain.

4. *It should be targeted at imbalanced trading relationships.* In 2012 the United States ran a more than twenty billion dollar trade surplus in goods with Australia. Australia clearly is not part of the U.S. trade balance problem, so targeting Australia in any way would be gratuitous and counter-productive in the effort to balance trade.

The next several chapters assess strategies that aim to balance trade. We will evaluate a range of proposals on the extent to which they are: (1) effective, (2) efficient, (3) legal, and (4) targeted. In chapter 8, we will discuss a range of ideas that have been proposed as possible solutions to the U.S. trade deficits. In chapter 9, we will discuss the Scaled Tariff, a proposal that we invented in order to satisfy all four criteria.

8

Methods for Balancing Trade

This chapter begins our evaluation of policies aimed at improving the U.S. balance of trade. We begin with the method utilized by recent U.S. presidents.

WHY TALKING DOWN THE TRADE DEFICIT FAILS

In December 2006, just after the Republican Party lost control of both the House and the Senate, often in races where Democrats raised trade and outsourcing as issues, the Bush administration woke up to the fact that their failure to deal with Chinese mercantilism could cost their party the 2008 election.

So that month President Bush sent all of the government's top financial leaders to China (Treasury Secretary Henry Paulson, Federal Reserve Chairman Ben S. Bernanke, Secretary of Commerce Carlos Gutierrez, Labor Secretary Elaine Chao, and Health and Human Services Secretary Mike Leavitt) to emphasize that we were serious this time. Unfortunately, their primary policy approach was ineffective.

By sending so many top officials to China at the same time, Bush was doubling down on the United States' favorite strategy for addressing mercantilist trading partners and imbalanced trade—pressuring one country (China today, Japan in the late 1980s) to change policy. But attempting to talk mercantilists out of mercantilism tends to produce modest results at best. They wouldn't be pursuing their current policies if they didn't think those policies served their interests.

According to the close reading of the communiqué afterward (Trippon 2006), the Bush mission was an abject failure. If it could not get Chinese cooperation, the Bush administration hinted that it would file a complaint with the World Trade Organization. Indeed, a few months later, U.S. trade representative Sue Schwabb filed two WTO complaints against China (Kavilanz 2007).

In addition, Bush's treasury secretary pressured the Chinese government into raising the yuan–dollar exchange rate, but the slight change in the exchange rate that resulted was not nearly enough to turn around the growing U.S. trade deficit with China. China was getting so much more investment in its manufacturing industries than the United States that its trade surplus with the United States continued to expand, despite the slight appreciation of the yuan.

By the time President Obama got elected in 2008, it was already clear that talking China into gradually strengthening its exchange rate would not balance trade. Nevertheless, the Obama administration continued to try to persuade China to do so. Although there have been periodic hints that China may change its policies and diminish its currency manipulations, none of these efforts have significantly altered the trajectory of the U.S.–China trade imbalance. Gradual revaluation may have marginally reduced the quantity demanded, but the combined factors of increased productivity, higher import barriers, and higher prices kept the value of China's surplus with the United States growing.

Talking mercantilists out of mercantilism won't work if mercantilism seems to be working. When exploiting U.S. cooperation provides benefits to the mercantilist, there is little reason for them to significantly change course. Thus, the benefits of talk, if unalloyed with stronger strategies, are likely to be minimal. Talk won't work unless combined with substantial and credible threats.

WHY THE CURRENCY RATE REFORM BILLS ARE INSUFFICIENT

During recent years, Congress has proposed but not passed currency rate reform bills. For example, during the 2009–2010 Congress, a *Currency Exchange Rate Oversight Reform Bill* was introduced by Senator Charles Schumer and a *Currency Reform for Fair Trade Act* was introduced by Representative Timothy Ryan. The House bill passed the Democratic House, but was then tabled by the Democratic Senate. During the 2011–2012 session, the Senate bill passed the Democratic Senate but was tabled by the Republican House.

Each bill had a different method for determining whether a country was manipulating its currency and the extent of those manipulations. The Senate bill relied upon the treasury secretary to make that determination, while the House bill relied upon statistics that are voluntarily reported by governments to international organizations. Both bills provided for the U.S. Commerce Department to assess the amount that a currency is overvalued when deciding individual industry by industry anti-dumping and countervailing duty suits.

Neither of the bills contained provisions likely to effectively balance trade. If either bill were to pass, the result would at-best be more suits on the Commerce Department's docket that would be expensive and time consuming for each individual industry to put together and for the Commerce Department to adjudicate. Any tariffs that would be applied would be piecemeal, not across the board. In response, trading partners would likely impose counter-tariffs.

Recent experience suggests that the result would have minimal effect. In March 2002, President Bush unilaterally imposed a temporary anti-dumping tariff on steel. The tariff was mainly targeted at Japan, China, and Europe. But on November 11, 2003, the WTO came out against the tariff and the European Union announced that it would impose retaliatory tariffs, so Bush withdrew them.

From September 26, 2009, to September 26, 2012, President Obama imposed a temporary tariff on Chinese tires that was authorized by China's agreement with the United States when it entered the World Trade Organization. Although the WTO supported the suit, China imposed a 36 percent counter-tariff on U.S. nylon products.

Piecemeal anti-dumping suits won't solve the U.S. trade deficit. Prosecution of currency manipulation on an industry-by-industry basis invites industry-by-industry retaliation. The United States has rarely demonstrated the fortitude or persistence required to win such confrontations, even when supported by the WTO. Thus, the currency rate reform legislation is unlikely to be effective at balancing trade with China or the world.

Finally, it is not clear whether the currency reform bills would be consistent with WTO rules. They would be imposed under anti-dumping provisions even though the WTO has not yet recognized that currency manipulation qualifies as dumping. It is possible, but not likely, that if such bills passed they would get the mercantilist countries to end their currency manipulations. But much more likely, they would only help those industries that could afford the anti-dumping suits, and they would likely hurt U.S. agriculture and other U.S. exporters as a result of counter-tariffs.

THE CHALLENGES OF IMPOSING AN UNCONDITIONAL TARIFF

In his book, *Free Trade Doesn't Work: What Should Replace It and Why*, Ian Fletcher (2010) came up with three proposals for balancing trade. Each of them was an improvement over the piecemeal approach of the currency bills in the sense that it would have a larger chance of actually moving trade toward balance.

Fletcher's featured proposal was a Natural Strategic Tariff, a flat tariff in the range of 25–30 percent. This tariff would apply equally to every good and service entering the country, no matter whether it was arriving from Canada or China. He claimed that the tariff would work because "Industries differ in their sensitivity and response to import competition." A 30 percent tariff would not restore the clothing industry but would restore high-tech manufacturing like semiconductors.

Fletcher acknowledged that the sudden imposition of a tariff in the 25 to 30 percent range could cause instability, so he suggested that the tariff be phased in gradually. He suggested that domestic producers benefitting from the imposition of the tariff might take undue advantage of the protection they receive and become inefficient monopolies, but believed that problem could be dealt with.

A major limitation of Fletcher's Natural Strategic Tariff is its inability to distinguish between countries that are running large trade deficits with the United States and countries running large trade surpluses. It provides no incentive for countries to avoid retaliating against U.S. exporters. It would also directly violate the current rules of international trade. As a result, it risks creating a retaliatory spiral that reduces global trade and welfare, but fails to procure the benefits of balanced trade. Ultimately the goal should be to reach an outcome that expands world trade, not a protectionist spiral.

A number of other authors have proposed more or less unconditional imposition of tariffs on particular countries as a way to combat the trade deficit. For example, in 2010 Nobel Prize-winning trade economist Paul Krugman called for a 25 percent tariff to counterbalance China's currency manipulations. He was suggesting that the tariff rate should be proportional to the amount that the Chinese currency is undervalued. In the March 14 issue of the *New York Times*, Krugman (2010) wrote:

> In 1971 the United States dealt with a similar but much less severe problem of foreign undervaluation by imposing a temporary 10 percent surcharge on imports, which was removed a few months later after Germany, Japan and other nations raised the dollar value of their currencies. At this point, it's hard to see China changing its policies unless faced with the threat of similar action—except that this time the surcharge would have to be much larger, say 25 percent.

Krugman dismissed widespread defeatism concerning Chinese retaliation, arguing that America has little to fear from China dumping U.S. assets because such action would make American products more competitive. He was definitely on the right track. However, China's trade manipulations involve much more than just currency manipulations. China could retaliate, for example, through tariff and non-tariff barriers to American products.

In order to prevent such retaliation, the tariff rate should be announced as being proportional to U.S.–China trade deficits, as outlined in the Scaled Tariff proposal in the next chapter. Not only are trade deficits a concrete measure, but they also give the tariff legitimacy since there is a special WTO rule which lets trade deficit countries apply import limitations or duties in order to balance trade.

With this mechanism in place, if our trade deficit with China would come down, the tariff rate would also come down. If our trade deficit with China goes up, the tariff rate would go up. If our trade with China reaches relative balance, the tariff would disappear.

THE VIRTUES OF A VAT OR SALES TAX

Fletcher (2010) also proposed a 25–30 percent VAT (value-added tax) in order to shift trade toward balance. The effect of a VAT upon the economy is economically identical to the effect of a sales tax. Both are "border adjustable," which means that they are imposed upon imports but not on exports. Almost all U.S. trading partners already impose significant value-added taxes on imports from the United States and rebate value added taxes on their exports, a policy permitted under current global trade rules.

The U.S. dependence on income taxes places U.S. producers at a disadvantage in international competition. U.S. produced goods sold abroad are taxed twice (domestic income taxes and foreign value-added taxes) while foreign goods sold in the United States may be almost tax free (low foreign income taxes, and rebated value-added taxes).

A VAT could also facilitate significant U.S. tax reform. The President's Advisory Panel on Federal Tax Reform (2005) calculated that a 15 percent VAT, made progressive at low income levels through work and family credits, would collect 65 percent of the revenue then collected by the personal and corporate income taxes combined. Thus a 25 to 30 percent VAT could be more than sufficient to eliminate the U.S. personal and corporate income taxes altogether!

Another advantage of the VAT is that it is both less expensive to collect and less expensive to comply with than the income tax. Individual taxpayers would not pay it, and, thus, would not have to spend time filling out tax returns. Businesses would pay it on the value of the products that they have sold after subtracting the value of the products that they have purchased from other businesses. The current U.S. tax code involves compliance costs of 12 to 15 percent, but the European compliance costs of the VAT, according to the same presidential commission, are just 3 to 5 percent of the tax collected.

Although the VAT is a flat tax, its burden on the poor and middle class could be reduced by offering a prebate, as in the FairTax (Boortz and Linder 2005), a national sales tax. A prebate, sufficient to pay the VAT on necessities, could go to all families in proportion to the number of adults and children in the family. In addition, because the VAT is a tax on consumption (it leaves savings untaxed) it would encourage Americans to save more money, and those savings would replace the foreign savings coming into the United States, keeping American interest rates low as trade moves towards balance.

Alternatively, a VAT on goods could be used to replace the corporate income tax, a tax which violates nearly every criterion of a good tax. It is expensive to administer and to comply with. It violates the principle that persons with equal incomes and circumstances should bear an equal burden, and it causes corporations to engage in uneconomic practices, including relying too heavily on debt financing.[1]

Arnold Harberger (2006), renowned expert on the incidence of the corporate income tax, found that corporations which compete only against domestic products are often able to pass the tax forward to consumers or backward to their employees, but that manufacturers of tradable goods usually cannot pass the tax forward to consumers because of international competition, so the corporate income tax mainly reduces manufacturing investment and labor compensation. In contrast, the VAT applies equally to foreign and domestic goods, so it is passed forward to consumers.

The VAT is definitely a good proposal, especially if it replaces the corporate income tax, but it shares a problem with the Natural Strategic Tariff. It doesn't stop trade from readjusting through a change in exchange rates. The mercantilist countries, especially, could manipulate their currency exchange rates by the same percentage as the tariff or VAT, unless successful restrictions on foreign asset purchases accompanied the VAT.

Also, the VAT does not specifically target mercantilist countries. Mercantilist countries could continue to exclude American exports, taking away investment opportunities from American manufacturing. Without investment opportunities, corporations wouldn't invest, even if the corporate income tax were eliminated.

THE ROLE OF RESTRICTIONS ON FOREIGN ASSET PURCHASES

Another approach to tackling the trade deficit is to directly target those financial inflows that finance trade deficits. If not for them, excess dollars paid for exports would bid down the dollar in foreign exchange markets, and the lower dollar would eventually balance trade. Although China uses capital controls to prevent a backwash of private savings when they force Chinese savings into the United States, the United States fails to use capital controls to keep out Chinese savings. It is about time that we did so.

Fletcher (2010) proposed addressing the problem of mercantilist purchases of U.S. financial assets by prohibiting such purchases or by taxing profits earned from such purchases. He wrote:

> China's currency is manipulated relative to our own *only because we permit it*, as there is no law requiring us to sell China our bonds and other assets. We can, in fact, end this manipulation at will. All we would need to do is bar China's purchases or tax them to death. (p. 74–75)

One challenge with Fletcher's suggestion is enforcement. Foreign governments often invest in the United States using international banks as intermediaries. We don't know about most of the Chinese investments in the United States. As far as we can tell, their assets are held in "eurodollar" accounts by banks in Singapore, Hong Kong, and Europe. Governments hide behind street names knowing that we also let private foreigners earn U.S. interest tax-free. This issue could of course be partially addressed by reinstating the withholding tax on private foreign investment, which would require renegotiation of our tax treaties.

Thus it would be very difficult for us to even determine which investments in government bonds were purchased by foreign banks and which were purchased by foreign governments. We would have to prevent all foreigners from buying U.S. government securities, or tax all foreign investors heavily.

In addition, what's to stop foreigners from investing in American banks and buying assets using those investments? Furthermore, what is to stop foreign governments from directly or indirectly buying private American assets such as stocks and bonds that are sold on stock and bond exchanges. Additional restrictions would be needed.

The *New York Post* featured an excellent commentary by Diane Francis (2013) entitled, "Why are we letting China buy American companies?" It's about a Chinese company's purchase of U.S. pork producer Smithfield Foods of Virginia. Francis predicts the following:

> The Smithfield buyout is a great loss because the company has become a huge exporter, to Japan and elsewhere, and has developed, with taxpayer assistance, systems and technologies that are best in class. . . .
>
> The damage includes the fact that Smithfield's technology, research and development, and patents will be transferred to the Chinese parent company. Smithfield will be hollowed out and the head office will be moved to China. Talent will leave.

Francis's concern about the loss of American technology is valid and important. And there is another important concern. Financial flows of capital into the United States, such as this, do not benefit the United States in the long-run. They drive up the dollar versus the yuan in world markets which makes American producers less competitive. They cause asset price bubbles which later burst. Any benefits are temporary, at best.

Instead of trying to stop the inflow of financial capital, the United States tax code actually subsidizes the inflow of financial capital by granting two special tax loopholes: (1) exempting non-resident foreigners from paying tax on interest earned, and (2) exempting foreign governments from paying tax even on dividends earned. We have advocated closing these loopholes (Richman, Richman, and Richman 2008). Regarding the loophole which exempts non-resident foreigners from paying U.S. taxes on interest earned in the United States, we wrote:

> If we delete §871(h,i,k) and §881(c,d,e) from the Internal Revenue Service code and either terminate or renegotiate our tax treaties with foreign governments, private foreigners would soon pay a 30% withholding tax on any interest earned in the United States on their financial investments. Almost all of these treaties include a provision that they can be terminated unilaterally by either country. As a result, they are very easy to renegotiate. When we renegotiate these treaties, they should be restructured to eliminate all limitations on our taxation of interest paid by Americans to nonresident foreigners. (p. 90–91)

Regarding the exemption from U.S. taxes on interest and dividends earned by foreign governments we wrote:

> The United States should tax dollar mercantilism by placing the highest rate of tax possible on foreign government investments. If it were possible, we would tax foreign government investments at a 100 percent rate so that they would earn no interest or

> dividends whatsoever. We would also make it completely illegal for foreign governments to buy stock in U.S. corporations, as they are currently doing through their Sovereign Wealth Funds. U.S. capitalism should not be for sale! (p. 101)

Taxing foreign investment is a more promising approach than banning it outright. At minimum, policies that provide foreign savings with advantageous rates relative to domestic savings should be ended.

One class of investment from mercantilist countries should not be targeted, however. It would be very different if a Chinese company were building a new factory in the United States as opposed to purchasing existing U.S. companies or financial assets. Then they would be bringing something to the table that would benefit the American economy.

We could do much more than we are currently doing to tax foreign governments who buy U.S. assets as part of their mercantilist strategies, but it is almost impossible to stop them from buying U.S. assets altogether. As Adam Smith documented in *Wealth of Nations*, Spain tried fighting British and French mercantilism by trying to stop the outflow of its gold (the foreign asset that the mercantilists of the sixteenth and seventeenth centuries sought), but its efforts failed. It is much easier to stop the smuggling of goods than it is to stop transfers of money.

Ultimately, tax policy may simply not be effective at discouraging mercantilism. The Chinese government doesn't send its savings to the United States in order to get high returns; it could get a higher return in China. It does so in order to maintain its trade surplus with the United States.

THE ROLE AND LIMITS OF COUNTERVAILING CURRENCY INTERVENTIONS

Bergsten and Gagnon (2012) of the Peterson Institute for International Economics proposed that the United States engage in countervailing currency interventions to balance trade. They explained:

> CCI is a simple concept. The European Central Bank, for example, could buy as many Swiss francs against euros as the Swiss National Bank (SNB) had sold against euros. This should neutralize any net impact on the exchange rate between the two currencies. (p. 17)

They pointed out that CCI poses little risk of the Federal Reserve or the U.S. Treasury losing money, since in most cases they would be buying currencies that were undervalued that could be sold later, when they would presumably rise to their trade-balancing exchange rates.

However, CCI's would not be possible with all countries. In fact, Bergsten and Gagnon point out that the chief currency manipulator, China, severely limits foreign purchases of its reserves, so Bergsten and Gagnon urge that the United States should, in such cases, "restrict or tax their purchases of dollar assets" instead (p. 17). Counter currency interventions only work when the trading partner has deep enough and open enough financial markets.

Aside from the difficulty of using CCI to tackle the massive trade deficit with China, interventions that are matched to foreign government interventions depend upon data reporting from foreign governments, which would have an incentive to distort their reports. Central banks only report currency conversions and reserve purchases voluntarily. Many do not report the currency composition of their reserves, and many do not report the stock and bond purchases by their sovereign wealth funds. Furthermore, central banks can hide their purchases by channeling them through private banks.

Also, it is much easier for a trade surplus country to engage in currency purchases. It buys foreign currency from its exporters and then "sterilizes" it from foreign exchange markets. The central bank of a trade deficit country has more limited access to foreign currency.

THE DIFFICULTIES OF REACHING INTERNATIONAL AGREEMENT

During World War II, John Maynard Keynes tried to insure future balanced trade by creating an international institution that would require it. Even though he did not have an official position in the British government, he was so influential as a consultant to the British Treasury Department that he was chosen to be Britain's chief negotiator at the July 1944 Bretton Woods conference which established the International Monetary Fund (IMF).

Under Keynes's proposal, the IMF would have instead been an "International Clearing Union" which would establish an international settlement currency (the *bancor*) and keep trade in balance. Volume 25 of his collected writings (Keynes 1980) is full of his plans for the fund which was to enshrine balanced trade as its primary goal using the *bancor* to insure balance. Trade surplus countries would be required to reduce their trade surplus through:

> (a) measures for the expansion of domestic credit and domestic demand;
> (b) the appreciation of its local currency in terms of *bancor*, or, if preferred, an increase in money wages;
> (c) the reduction of excessive tariffs and other discouragements against imports;
> (d) international loans for the development of backward countries. (pp. 79–80)

Meanwhile, *only* trade deficit countries would be permitted to subsidize exports and place barriers on imports through any of the following actions:

> (i) restrictions on the disposal of receipts . . .
> (ii) import restrictions, whether quantitative or in the form of "duty quotas" (excluding, however, prohibitions designed to safeguard, e.g., public health or morals or revenue collection);

(iii) barter arrangements (providing one party to the agreement is a deficit country and the same arrangement with the deficit country is available to others);
(iv) export quotas and discriminatory export taxes;
(v) export subsidies either furnished directly by the state or indirectly under schemes supported or encouraged by the state; and
(vi) excessive tariffs. (p. 80–81)

Unfortunately, Keynes was opposed at every turn of the Bretton Woods negotiations by chief U.S. negotiator Harry Dexter White, a Soviet spy in the U.S. Treasury Department who may have wanted to weaken Britain (Skidelski 2000, 263). Also, the United States, as a major trade surplus country, was reluctant to endorse policies that could threaten its trade balance. White's counter-proposal for an "International Stabilization Fund" became the basis for the IMF.

We will never know how well Keynes proposal would have worked. Keynes was a brilliant economist, the negotiators of America's trade agreements less so. Both China's accession to the WTO (chapter 5) and the Korea–U.S. free trade agreement (chapter 1) immediately worsened the U.S. trade deficits.

The IMF's Articles of Agreement sounded good on paper. To this day, Article IV requires that countries "avoid manipulating exchange rates or the international monetary system in order to prevent effective balance of payments adjustment or to gain an unfair competitive advantage over other members." But that provision is usually ignored. Keynes faith in international institutions was, perhaps, misplaced. Only trade deficit countries can be trusted to balance trade, because it is to their benefit to do so.

BUFFETT'S IMPORT CERTIFICATES

Financier and businessman Warren Buffett first proposed Import Certificates (ICs) to balance trade in a 2003 *Fortune Magazine* article. His proposal may have been modeled upon the "cap-and-trade" plans that had successfully reduced pollution, but instead his plan would cap imports to the level of exports, thereby balancing trade. Buffett and Loomis (2003) wrote:

> We would achieve this balance by issuing what I will call Import Certificates (ICs) to all U.S. exporters in an amount equal to the dollar value of their exports. Each exporter would, in turn, sell the ICs to parties—either exporters abroad or importers here—wanting to get goods into the United States. To import $1 million of goods, for example, an importer would need ICs that were the byproduct of $1 million of exports. The inevitable result: trade balance.

Under the Buffett plan, whenever American producers exported American products abroad, they would earn ICs that they could profitably sell to prospective importers. Meanwhile, imports would face the additional cost of the required ICs.

In September 2006, Senators Byron Dorgan and Russ Feingold fleshed out the Buffett plan into bill form, which they named the *Balanced Trade Restoration Act of 2006*. Their bill would have the Department of Commerce issue ICs (which they called "Balanced Trade Certificates") directly to exporters.

Each $1 of exports (based upon the appraised value declared on the shipper's export declaration) would earn the exporter a $1 IC which the exporter could then freely market to those who wished to import goods into the United States, and the Commerce Department would require that the certificates be submitted with imports. The value of imports allowed by an IC would change over time. During the first year of the program, a $1 certificate would allow up to $1.40 of imports, during the second year, $1.30 of imports, the third year $1.20, and so on until by the fifth year $1 of exports would allow $1 of imports.

The Buffett plan provided a guaranteed path to balanced trade and the additional benefit of providing subsidies to exporters from the sale of the ICs. In a commentary endorsing Buffett's plan, Ralph Gomory (2010) pointed out that balancing trade and rewarding productivity are the two components that are needed in order for a country to recover industries that it has been losing due to manipulations of manufacturing comparative advantages.

In a 2008 Levy Economics Institute working paper, Dimitri B. Papadimitriou, Greg Hannsgen, and Gennaro Zezza analyzed the costs and benefits of the Buffett plan, making quantitative estimates of the effects. They pointed out that the Buffett plan would cause an immediate macroeconomic boost to the economy, increase profits of businesses that produce for export, increase government tax collections (because of increased American income), and reduce trade deficits to a sustainable level.

But one limitation of the Buffett plan, according to international lawyers Stewart and Drake (2009, 11), is that the provision of marketable ICs to exporters could lead to "potential inconsistencies with WTO prohibitions on export subsidies." Another limitation is that it targets all countries equally, whether or not they are running deficits or surpluses. As a result, it imposes costs on U.S. trading partners who are not mercantilist, and thereby risks providing insufficient incentives for mercantilist trading partners to alter their behavior.

COUNTRY-SPECIFIC IMPORT CERTIFICATES

In an effort to address these two limitations, we developed a targeted IC plan (Richman, Richman, and Richman 2008) in which the ICs would be auctioned by the government and would be country-specific. The targeted ICs were designed to gradually balance trade over a five year period with countries that practice mercantilism, as evidenced by excessive foreign exchange reserve accumulations by their governments. Certificates would be auctioned in the open market and expire in six months. Each certificate would permit a certain value of imports from the targeted country as a multiple of its exports. The ratio of imports to exports would gradually diminish over a period of five years to bring trade toward balance.

A key advantage of country-specific Import Certificates is that they preclude trade retaliation because countries are assessed on the basis of their trade balance. If a mercantilist government were to respond with counter-restrictions of its own, it would be directly reducing the amount of its own exports to the country issuing the certificates. If imposed, targeted ICs take the unequal cooperate/exploit equilibrium of the game of chicken (chapter 7) off the table, making cooperation the dominant strategy.

Administrative costs and uncertainty are the major challenges with IC plans, although neither is insurmountable. The two IC plans require that a new government bureaucracy be set up to administer the ICs. In addition, they add a new cost to businesses, the cost of obtaining the ICs in order to obtain imports. Papadimitriou et al. argue that these costs would produce significant uncertainty on the part of businesses needing imported products. But importers and exporters already deal with future uncertainty in foreign trade due to changing exchange rates. Furthermore, both IC plans would place expiration dates upon the ICs so that the futures market for ICs would be liquid.

Papadimitriou et al. also pointed out that if, as under the Buffett plan, ICs could be earned by service exports, not just goods exports, this would create a large incentive to fraudulently obtain ICs from intra-corporate transactions. The Targeted IC plan avoids this problem because it does not provide export subsidies.

Like the Buffett plan, the targeted IC plan would revive exporting industries by increasing exports, although the plan does not provide the direct subsidies associated with the Buffett plan. If the mercantilist governments refused to increase their imports, then the trade deficit country would increase its imports from countries that themselves import more when their economy grows.

CONCLUSION

Among the policies discussed so far, one of the best is implementation of a VAT or consumption tax paired with the elimination of the corporate income tax. This would put U.S. producers on a more equal footing with international competitors. Also well worth considering are policies that place taxes on foreign capital, ending the preferential treatment currently given to foreign savers and reducing the extent to which private financial flows produce trade deficits. Counter Currency Interventions are also a promising idea as they could somewhat reverse the flow of government savings into the United States. But, the Import Certificate proposals offer the surest route to balanced trade by explicitly conditioning their application on the trade balance.

The next chapter develops in detail a tariff policy that also explicitly conditions its application on the balance of trade. The Scaled Tariff is closely related to the IC plans, but its use of tariffs instead of import certificates reduces uncertainty and enforcement costs. It is designed to balance trade surely and efficiently without punishing non-mercantilist trading partners and without violating World Trade Organization rules.

NOTE

1. Replacing the Corporate Income Tax with a VAT would necessitate two additional changes in the tax code in order to preserve the tax code's progressivity and in order to prevent corporations from being used to convert income into lower taxed capital gains. First, dividends and capital gains would have to be taxed as normal income, not given a special rate. Second, in order to avoid taxation of capital, capital gains taxation should be deferred through the rollover treatment (Richman, Richman, and Richman 2008, chapter 5) whenever capital is rolled over from one asset to another.

9

The Scaled Tariff

The Scaled Tariff is a single-country variable tariff whose rate rises as the trade deficit increases and falls as trade becomes more balanced. It is a tariff upon all the goods being imported by a trade deficit country from a trade-surplus country. No particular product is protected; the Scaled Tariff simply changes the terms of trade between the two countries much as currency devaluation would change the terms of trade with all countries.

By targeting countries with which the United States has a large trade deficit, the Scaled Tariff would efficiently, legally, and effectively balance trade. It would be applied to all imported goods from trade surplus countries that have had a sizable trade surplus with the United States over the most recent four economic quarters. The tariff rate would be designed to take in 50 percent of the bilateral trade deficit (goods plus services) as revenue.

FORBEARS OF THE SCALED TARIFF

The first bill that would have required balanced trade was introduced by Democratic Congressman and future Majority Leader Dick Gephart and by Senators Carl Levin and Donald Riegel in 1985 and 1987. As originally written, Gephardt's bill would have required the following:

1. The International Trade Commission (ITC) would identify any country that: (a) had a total U.S. bilateral trade of seven billion dollars or more, (b) had a total bilateral non-petroleum surplus of three billion dollars or more, and (c) exported 1.75 times more non-petroleum products to the United States than it imported;

2. The United States Trade Representative (USTR) would determine whether the above "excessive surplus" countries maintained "unjustifiable, unreasonable, or discriminatory" trade practices that adversely affected U.S. commerce and contributed to their trade surpluses;
3. The USTR would enter negotiations for sixty days (sixty day extension) with each country identified in steps 1 and 2. The purpose of negotiations would be to achieve an annual 10 percent reduction in trade surplus from the preceding year;
4. If the USTR were unable to enter such an agreement, then the president would take any of the actions specified that he considers "necessary or appropriate." If action in the first year did not achieve the reductions, then the president would be required to limit imports to achieve the reductions;
5. The president could (a) allow less than a 10 percent reduction in surplus, if the other country had balance of payments difficulties; or (b) waive presidential retaliation, if such action would harm the national economic interest. In each case, the president would have to submit an alternative plan to Congress. Congress could disallow the president's decision by joint resolution.

Proponents of Gephardt's provisions argued that they correctly targeted the largest and worst trade offenders, Japan and other countries that had intentionally produced large trade surpluses with the United States through unfair trade practices that kept out American products. They noted that it would not place any barriers upon the products of those countries with which the United States has little trade or balanced trade.

In 1987, Gephart's proposal was added, with slight modifications, to H.R. 3, by the House Ways and Means Committee. However, according to a Congressional Research Service Report, the Reagan administration threatened to veto H.R. 3 unless the Gephart Amendment were withdrawn because it "contemplate(s) a balancing of bilateral trade through trade policy actions rather than addressing the problem of large external balances through macroeconomic policies."

Also, the Reagan administration argued that the Gephart Amendment would violate GATT, the predecessor to the World Trade Organization, as well as the economic theory which holds that exchange rates balance trade, making such measures unnecessary.

In 1987 one could perhaps be excused for thinking that exchange rates would balance trade. The recently developed Plaza Accord had substantially reduced the exchange rate of the U.S. dollar, and this was partially rebalancing U.S. trade with Western Europe. The trade deficit with Japan, however, turned out to be resistant to these measures. The goods trade deficit with Japan was forty-six billion dollars in 1985 when the Plaza Accord was reached, and remained above that level throughout the ensuing decades with the exception of the U.S. recession years of 1990–1991 and 2009. As the experience with Japan shows, balancing trade with mercantilist trading partners requires stronger measures. It is a pity that Gephart's idea wasn't given a try.

Another forebear of our Scaled Tariff proposal was put forward in 2008 by University of Maryland business professor Peter Morici (2008), a former director of the Office of Economics at the U.S. International Trade Commission. He was the first to propose a tariff whose rate would go up or down depending upon actions that cause a trade deficit. He proposed a dollar–yuan conversion tax that would be applied to Chinese imports into the United States at a rate that would be adjusted to the rate of Chinese currency market interventions. He wrote:

> China subsidizes exports by selling its currency, the yuan, for dollars at artificially low values in foreign-exchange markets, making Chinese goods artificially cheap at Wal-Mart. The U.S. government should tax dollar–yuan conversions at a rate equal to China's subsidy until China stops manipulating currency markets. That would reduce imports from, and increase exports to, China.

Our proposal differs sharply from Morici's in targeting the trade deficit as the key indicator. We preferred trade data to currency conversion data because the central bank that is involved in currency market interventions may or may not choose to report them. China, for example, only reports the overall value of its foreign exchange reserves to international organizations, not the currency composition of its reserves, and it doesn't report the purchases of foreign assets by its sovereign wealth fund.

A TARIFF DESIGNED TO BALANCE TRADE

We first proposed the Scaled Tariff in a commentary for *Enter Stage Right* (Richman et al. 2010a). Then we elaborated upon it in a commentary for the *American Thinker* (Richman et al. 2010b), in written testimony for the House Ways and Means Committee (Richman et al. 2010c) and in a journal article that appeared in *The Estey Centre Journal of International Law and Trade Policy* (Richman et al. 2011).

Independently, Joseph Hitselberger (2011) came up with a similar idea which he called the "Proportional Tariff" in a July 30, 2011, commentary. He wrote:

> The solution is a proportional tariff. Tariffs should be applied to a country proportionately to the trade surplus they run with the United States. On a sliding scale, a country that has such a huge trade surplus with the United States should be given a 100 percent tariff (at least), while a friendly country (ally) that has an even balance of trade with the United States does not need a tariff at all.

With the Scaled Tariff, the United States would simply charge a tariff at the appropriate duty rates upon imported goods from the trade surplus countries.

The specifics of the Scaled Tariff, if enacted by the United States, would be the following:

1. *Applied only to trade surplus countries.* The tariff would only be applied to products of countries that had an overall trade surplus in goods of at least 1

percent of its GDP, which had a trade surplus in goods and services with the United States of at least one billion dollars over the most recent four quarters, and whose exports to the United States (goods plus services) were more than 110 percent of its imports from the United States (goods plus services) during the most recent four quarters.

2. *Applied only to goods.* The Commerce Department would charge the Scaled Tariff on all goods originating from each trade surplus country. The rate would be applied upon the declared dollar value of such goods on the entry summary form.
3. *Rate of duty designed to take in 50 percent of trade deficit.* The rate of the duty would be adjusted quarterly and calculated as the rate that would cause the revenue taken in by the duty upon imported goods from the particular country to equal 50 percent of the trade deficit (goods plus services) with that country over the most recent four economic quarters. The rate of the duty would be updated quarterly.
4. *Rebated to exporters.* The Commerce Department would rebate Scaled Tariff payments to U.S. exporters to the extent that they were paid on inputs to those particular exports.
5. *Suspended when trade reaches balance.* The Scaled Tariff would be suspended whenever the Commerce Department determined that during the most recent calendar year the current account of the United States was in surplus. Collection would resume when the Commerce Department determined that during the most recent calendar year the current account deficit of the United States was at least 1 percent of U.S. GDP.

THE SCALED TARIFF IN PRACTICE

Here's how the numbers of the Scaled Tariff would work with China in a particular year. In 2012 the United States imported $440 billion of goods and services from China, while China imported $112 billion of goods and services from the United States, creating a trade deficit of $298 billion. An initial tariff rate of 35 percent on $427 billion of imported goods from China would be designed to collect $149 billion (50 percent of $298 billion) in tariff revenue.

Goldstein (2007) concluded, after a careful study of the yuan's valuation, that it was 30 percent undervalued against most currencies and 40 percent undervalued as compared to the dollar, so a 35 percent tariff on Chinese products would be just about the right level.

The Commerce Department's Bureau of Economic Analysis (BEA) publishes complete goods and services trade statistics for some of America's trading partners, making it possible to calculate the Scaled Tariff rate for those countries. Based upon these 2012 data, the following rates would have been initially applied by the Scaled Tariff in 2013:

- China: 35 percent
- Japan: 20 percent

- Venezuela: 20 percent
- Euro-zone: 12 percent
- Taiwan: 12 percent
- South Korea: 7 percent

We would treat the euro-zone as a single country rather than as separate countries because its central bank could balance trade by selling off some of its extensive dollar reserves. Also, the euro-zone governments could stop subsidizing competition against American producers. For example, in July 2007 the European Commission approved Germany's gift of about $360 million to computer chip maker AMD to expand production in Dresden, Germany. Then on May 13, 2009, it fined AMD's chief competitor Intel €1.06 billion (about $1.45 billion) for alleged monopolistic abuses (Richman, Richman and Richman 2009).

Based upon 2012 data we estimate that a number of other countries would also have had the Scaled Tariff applied to their goods at the beginning of 2013 including:

- Denmark
- Gabon
- Kuwait
- Libya
- Malaysia
- Nigeria
- Norway
- Pakistan
- Philippines
- Russia
- Saudi Arabia
- Sweden
- Trinidad and Tobago
- Vietnam

Several of these countries, including Nigeria, Kuwait, Libya, Russia, Saudi Arabia, and Venezuela are oil exporters which do not import as much as they export. The Scaled Tariff would encourage them to increase their imports from the United States and/or to sell their oil elsewhere. In the meantime, the Scaled Tariff would encourage increased American oil production and greater use of America's plentiful natural gas as vehicle fuel.

THE SCALED TARIFF IS EFFECTIVE

The Scaled Tariff differs from the currency rate reform bills in that: (1) the determination of the tariff level is made from verifiable statistics, not just statistics that governments self-report, (2) the rate of the duty gets reduced as trade moves toward balance, and (3) the duty rate is applied across-the-board to all goods from a country.

Like the Buffett Import Certificate plan (Buffett and Loomis 2003) it provides a guaranteed path to balanced trade, but unlike the Buffett plan it only applies to those countries with which the United States is running a trade deficit. If the mercantilist governments refused to increase their imports, then the trade deficit country would increase its imports from countries that themselves import more when their economy grows.

It is inferior to the Buffett plan in that it does not provide export subsidies to the trade deficit country's exporting industries. However, the fact that it does not provide export subsidies makes the Scaled Tariff more compatible with WTO (World Trade Organization) rules than the Buffett plan.

After the Scaled Tariff is applied, the following events would occur:

- American imports from the trade-manipulating countries would decrease.
- American exports to the trade-manipulating countries would increase because they would reduce their trade manipulations.
- American imports from the non-manipulating countries would increase.
- American exports to the non-manipulating countries would increase, because their higher incomes would result in higher imports from the United States.

Other trade deficit countries would soon join the United States by enacting Scaled Tariffs of their own. The result would put world trade on a sustainable basis. Balanced trade can grow forever, but trade surpluses eventually bankrupt the trade deficit countries.

THE SCALED TARIFF IS EFFICIENT

None of the usual economic arguments against tariffs applies to the trade-balancing Scaled Tariff:

- It doesn't cause a trade war—countries that respond with counter-tariffs would be further increasing the U.S. tariff rate on their products which would discourage retaliation.
- It doesn't reduce exports—it causes trading partners to take down their barriers to U.S. exports and would likely increase U.S. exports.
- It doesn't hurt households—the new productive middle class jobs created by balancing trade would likely increase household incomes more than prices.
- It doesn't distort the economy—balanced trade is neutral with respect to GDP.
- It doesn't hurt the world economy—chronic trade deficits eventually cause financial crises because trade deficit countries must borrow from abroad to buy imports. Balanced trade can grow forever.

The Scaled Tariff is also superior to both of the Import Certificate plans discussed in chapter 8 in that: (1) it avoids the cost of setting up a new government bureaucracy to administer the certificates, (2) it avoids creating business uncertainty over availability of Import Certificates, and (3) it does not give businesses a direct incentive to fraudulently report intra-corporate transactions as service exports.

The administrative costs would be minimal; the Commerce Department would have to expand its collection and reporting of service trade data. It would also need to set up an office to compile country-by-country goods trade breakdowns that it would collect from foreign governments. The rest of the bill makes use of collection mechanisms that already exist.

LEGALITY UNDER INTERNATIONAL LAW

In an Economics Policy Institute working paper, Stewart and Drake (2009) discussed the legality of the various IC plans in terms of international law. Like the Scaled Tariff, the source of their legality is Article XII of GATT 1994, annexed to the Agreement Establishing the World Trade Organization. This framework permits any country that has (1) a perilous external financial position and (2) a balance of payments deficit in the current account to restrict the quantity or value of merchandise permitted to be imported in order to bring payments toward balance.

President Nixon made use of this rule when he imposed an across-the-board 10 percent tariff in August 1971 which quickly forced changes that brought U.S. trade into balance by 1973. Even though the United States was a net foreign creditor in 1971, IMF and GATT agreed that the United States had a perilous financial position simply because its reserves only equaled the value of about three months worth of imports. By this criteria, the United States continues to be in a perilous financial position. As Bergsten and Gagnon (2012, 11) noted: "U.S. foreign exchange reserves of $52 billion are tiny in comparison with standard metrics, such as three months of imports ($666 billion)."

The Scaled Tariff would meet the Article XII framework for many of the same reasons that Stewart and Drake noted would apply to the Import Certificate plans. Article XII expressly *permits* import duties that are in excess of the duties inscribed in the WTO schedule for a member and it *requires* that countries relax their import duties as the trade deficit grows smaller. The Scaled Tariff's rate goes down as trade with a country approaches balance and disappears entirely when bilateral trade approaches balance or the balance of payments in the U.S. current account reaches balance.

Furthermore, there is little reason to worry if WTO bureaucrats object. According to Bergsten and Gagnon, although the WTO has the ability to authorize trade restrictions against a country, the path to action is so "torturous . . . that it has never been tried let alone implemented" (p. 11). When President G. W. Bush enacted a steel tariff, he was forced to withdraw it not by the WTO ruling against it, but by the counter-tariffs that were enacted against the United States by the affected countries.

In contrast with Bush's steel tariff, the Scaled Tariff is nearly immune to counter-tariffs. Any country that enacts a counter-tariff would be increasing the U.S. tariff on its products. Instead of starting a trade war, the Scaled Tariff would provide automatic responses that would end the trade war that is currently being conducted upon the United States by the mercantilist countries. In terms of the game of chicken example developed in chapter 7, the Scaled Tariff is equivalent to a policy that automatically responds to the competitor's move with the identical move. In the face of such a policy, the response with highest payoffs for trading partners is to cooperate by reducing trade manipulations.

Retaliation against the value of the dollar would also be ineffective. If other countries were to rapidly sell their dollar holdings in response to the Scaled Tariff, doing so would just accelerate the trade balancing effects of the Scaled Tariff. Also, doing so would accelerate the countervailing movement of capital into the United States by international corporations rushing to locate new factories in the United States.

Furthermore, American net foreign debt is not *yet* so high that a withdrawal of foreign savings need be feared. If foreigners were to suddenly sell their American assets, the result, almost paradoxically, would be to make the net U.S. foreign debt easier to bear—declines in the dollar would raise the value of U.S. investments abroad while diminishing the value of dollar assets held by foreign investors. A timely repatriation of foreign profits and assets held by Americans (perhaps encouraged by tax incentives) could cushion dollar declines until an improved trade balance put a floor under the dollar.

THE SCALED TARIFF IS TARGETED

The Scaled Tariff specifically and exclusively targets countries which are running trade surpluses with the United States and with the world. Thus, it specifically creates incentives for these countries to take steps to shift their trade toward balance by stimulating their domestic economies, removing tariff and non-tariff barriers, ending currency manipulations, and so forth. It avoids targeting trade relations with countries that are not contributors to global current account imbalances.

Although the tariffs are targeted at trade surplus countries, they are not targeted at countries for any other reason. There is a GATT Article XII provision that prohibits targeting of specific countries. However, the Scaled Tariff is fairly set as the rate required to earn 50 percent of the value of the bilateral trade deficit with each trade surplus country. Thus it does not target specific countries in a way that violates WTO rules.

CONCLUSION

In the first year of the Scaled Tariff, the federal government would take in hundreds of billions of dollars of additional revenue, which would help balance the budget and increase U.S. savings rates. As the Scaled Tariff brought trade toward balance, tariff revenue would be replaced by increased revenue from higher American incomes. U.S. economic growth and median income growth would return to where they left off before trade deficits began to decimate both. The United States would experience a recovery much like the one that Great Britain experienced in 1933 and 1934 when it enacted the Imperial Preference System. And, as with the British action, U.S. policy would provide incentives for trading partners to reconsider and remove mercantilist policies that produce imbalanced trade.

10

Balanced Trade Economics

Congress's response to the Great Recession was borrowing for one failed stimulus package after another:

1. $152 billion Economic Stimulus Act in February 2008;
2. $862 billion American Recovery and Reinvestment Act February 2009;
3. Annual budget deficits over one trillion dollars in 2010, 2011, and 2012.

These economic stimuli were justified as an implementation of the Keynesian idea that when the government increases its budget deficit by a certain amount, GDP will increase by a multiple of that increased budget deficit. But none of these stimuli worked very well.

Take Obama's recovery plan of February 2009 (The American Recovery and Reinvestment Act). As shown in figure 10.1, the actual unemployment rate (the line with circles) actually fell more slowly than the unemployment rate was projected to decline if nothing were done (the plain line), according to two of President-elect Obama's top economic advisors (Romer and Bernstein 2009).

This chapter develops the implications of our analysis for macroeconomic theory and macroeconomic policy. We argue that each of the major perspectives on macroeconomic policy making (Keynesian, supply-side, and monetarist) needs to take more account of the balance of trade.

A balanced trade economics would recognize that spending, taxation, and monetary policy all influence the balance of trade, and that the balance of trade can mediate, undermine, or amplify the effectiveness of particular policy tools. In both fiscal and monetary policy, countries with trade deficits should make distinctly different policy choices than countries with trade surpluses.

Figure 10.1. Actual Unemployment Rate and Rate with No Stimulus

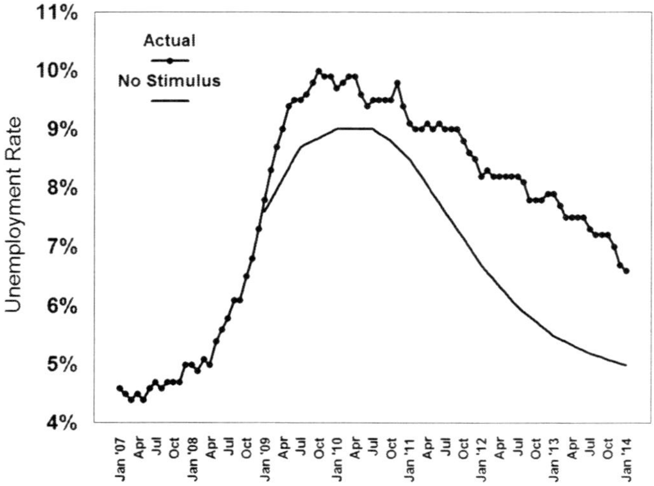

The actual unemployment rate is shown as the black line with circles on it in the graph. The gray line shows the predicted rate by Romer and Bernstein if Obama's Recovery Plan were not enacted. Sources: BLS and Romer and Bernstein (2009).

BALANCED TRADE KEYNESIANISM

Although it is possible that the stimulus plans failed because they were too small (Krugman 2012), or too badly crafted (Cogan and Taylor 2012), there was another reason why the Great Recession stimuli failed—the trade deficits. As we pointed out in chapter 1 (see our discussion of figure 1.4), President Obama's "recovery summer" failed to materialize despite growth in *C*onsumption, *I*nvestment, and *G*overnment Purchases (C + I + G), due to the simultaneous growth of the U.S. trade deficit, which subtracted from aggregate demand for the products of the economy.

Keynes thought that an increase in government purchasing or a tax cut would ripple through an economy at times of high unemployment. Each person receiving additional income would spend a proportion of it and each person receiving that proportion, would spend a proportion, and so on. As a result, the effect upon GDP during times of high unemployment would be several times the amount of the initial government purchase. Keynesians call this the "spending multiplier." It expresses the expected GDP increase as a multiple of the increase in government spending (other things being equal).

As a result Keynesian fiscal policy utilizes increases in government spending or decreases in tax collections to stimulate an economy during periods of unemployment. Liberal Keynesians tend to advocate increased government spending while their conservative counterparts (called "supply-side" economists) tend to advocate tax cuts. The February 2008 stimulus consisted of tax cuts and the February 2009 stimulus included tax cuts and spending, yet neither worked well. Perhaps this was because the multipliers simply were not very large. Major arguments persist about the size of the Keynesian multiplier, and indeed it appears to vary greatly depending upon the kind of spending applied (Ramey 2011), many modern estimates place it much lower than Keynes thought—below one, due to increases in government spending engendering decreases in private spending (Ramey 2013).[1]

In fairness to liberal Keynesians, the type of government spending utilized in the February 2009 stimulus was not the kind with the highest multiplier. Originally much of the money was to be spent on infrastructure which would have a high multiplier because it would reduce business costs. In a radio address, Obama (2008) referred to President Eisenhower's Interstate Highway System, one of the most successful infrastructure projects ever, as the model for his plan. He said:

> [W]e will create millions of jobs by making the single largest new investment in our national infrastructure since the creation of the federal highway system in the 1950s. We'll invest your precious tax dollars in new and smarter ways, and we'll set a simple rule—use it or lose it. If a state doesn't act quickly to invest in roads and bridges in their communities, they'll lose the money.

But throughout the legislative process, the amount of infrastructure investment kept going down, and when implemented, it went down even further. According to a careful analysis performed by Cogan and Taylor (2012) of how the stimulus money was actually spent, of the $862 billion in the plan only $0.9 billion in 2009 and $1.5 billion in the first quarters of 2010 were spent by the federal government on infrastructure

Another $137 billion of grants went to the states for infrastructure spending, but they reduced their borrowing by $105 billion and probably used it on projects that they would have done anyway. Cogan and Taylor explained that state governments, when they get temporary new revenue that they don't expect to continue, they tend to save it, not spend it. (This theory, when applied to individuals, is known to economists as Milton Friedman's Permanent Income Hypothesis.)

In fairness to supply-siders, the tax cuts passed in both stimulus plans were the least effective types possible. Instead of permanent tax cuts which people think will continue, they were temporary tax cuts, which the permanent income hypothesis suggests will nearly always fail. Take the $152 billion Bush Economic Stimulus Act of February 2008. There was no detectable increase in consumption, let alone in GDP, according to a careful analysis by John B. Taylor (2009).

When households get temporary new revenue that they don't expect to continue, many save most of it, not spend it. In contrast, according to a study of Bush's 2001 tax cut, about two-thirds of the tax rebates were soon spent on consumption (Johnson, Parker and Souleles 2006). They were effective, unlike the 2008 tax rebates, because they were part of a larger tax package that reduced tax rates over the long term, so households saw them as a relatively permanent change in income.[2]

We believe that the U.S. spending multiplier has gone down in recent years due to the persistent U.S. trade deficits. Stimulating an economy that has a large trade deficit is a bit like trying to pump up a flat tire without first fixing the leak. The faster you pump, the faster the stimulus leaks abroad. Some of this leakage results from consumers buying imports. Some results from direct government spending for foreign products, partly due to the increased power of importers that we discussed in chapter 5. For example, Prestowitz (2010, 5) relates that outsourcers lobbied to keep a "Buy America" provision out of Obama's Recovery Act:

> In a 2009 White House meeting, a group of top American CEO's who have offshored much of their production told President Obama that to prevent retaliation against U.S. exports he must avoid inclusion of any "buy American" provisions in his economic stimulus package even though the measures being considered were all perfectly legal and permissible under the rules of the World Trade Organization (WTO). Moreover, at that very moment, China, Japan, and most of the major European countries that might threaten retaliation were already implementing "buy domestic" policies of their own.

The foreign leakage concept was in some standard Keynesian models (e.g., Meade 1949; Gehrels 1960; Lim 2003), but is not mentioned in descriptions of the New Keynesian models (e.g., Cogan et. al. 2010). Imports detract from the aggregate demand for a country's goods while exports add to aggregate demand. Thus if a stimulus adds more to imports than it does to exports, the multiplier is reduced. Our hypothesis is that there are three trade conditions which affect the multiplier differently:

1. *Balanced trade.* We argue that when trade is and remains balanced, foreign leakage doesn't affect the multiplier. That's because when imports go up, exports soon follow due to a decline in the exchange rate and an increase in the income of trading partners.
2. *Trade surplus.* When a country is running a persistent trade surplus, it is manifestly clear that its currency value isn't adjusting to trade imbalances. A stimulus would increase demand for imports, which would stimulate export markets, causing an increase in exports that would counter or even outweigh the leakage abroad of the stimulus.
3. *Trade deficit.* When a country is running a persistent trade deficit, it is manifestly true that its currency value isn't adjusting to trade imbalances. In such a case, increased demand for imports, due to a stimulus, is *not* likely to engender an equivalent increase in its exports. As a result, a stimulus in a trade deficit country tends to result in more foreign leakage and a smaller multiplier effect.

As a result, increasing government purchases or lowering taxes should have a larger multiplier effect upon trade surplus countries and a lower effect upon trade deficit countries.

Keynes thought that recessions occurred during times when domestic businesses had too few investment opportunities for the amount of savings that a country was producing. He argued that a government can alleviate a recession by bringing savings down to the level of business investment. Modern economists implement Keynes's argument through fiscal and monetary policies:

- Modern fiscal policies reduce domestic savings through increased budget deficits (government dissavings).
- Modern monetary policies reduce domestic savings by buying privately owned bonds (which reduces interest rates or causes inflation).

However, Keynes (1936, 335) also noted that countries have a third option, the one utilized by mercantilists of transferring their savings abroad by running a trade surplus. Although Keynes did not say so explicitly, it follows that a country that is running a trade deficit can possibly end a recession by balancing trade, thus reversing the net inflow of excess foreign savings.

Balanced trade Keynesianism implies that budget deficits will be much less effective at stimulating the economies of trade deficit countries. To provide a preliminary test of this implication, we analyzed cross-sectional linear regression equations with an interaction between budget and current account variables for several recent years.

Figure 10.2. Differential Response to Budget Deficits

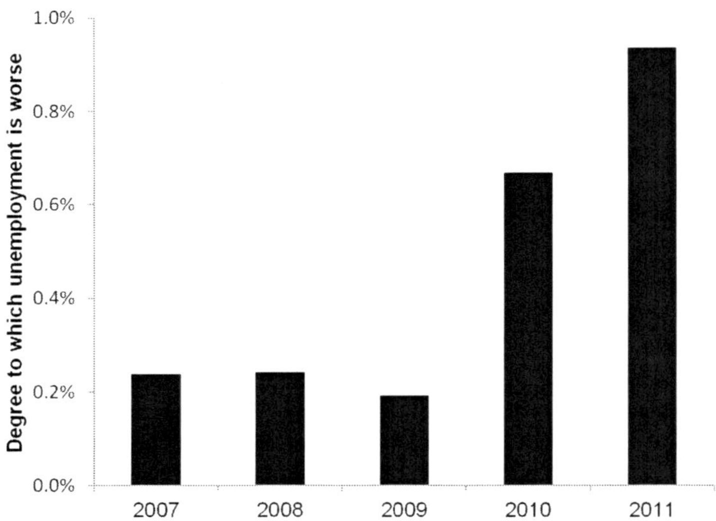

Our results suggest the degree to which unemployment would be worse in a trade deficit country as compared to a trade surplus country during the years shown. Source: author calculation based on analysis of data from Tradingeconomics.com.

For every year except 2009, this interaction achieved at least marginal levels of statistical significance ($p < 0.10$ two tailed) and in the expected direction.

The results were precisely as projected. The degree to which government deficit spending helps or harms a country's unemployment rate depends upon the balance of trade. As shown in figure 10.2, this means that in 2011, if both a country with a 10 percent trade deficit (analogous to Greece) and a country with a 10 percent trade surplus (analogous to Norway) were to increase their government budget deficits by 1 percent of GDP, the projected unemployment rate in the trade deficit country would be 0.93 percent worse compared to the unemployment rate in the trade surplus country. These results suggest that trade deficit countries derive less benefit from deficit spending than trade surplus countries.

How much would balancing trade help reduce U.S. unemployment? According to a simulation reported by Bergsten and Gagnon (2012, 5) of the Peterson Institute for International Economics using the Federal Reserve's FRB/US macroeconomic model of the U.S. economy, if the United States would eliminate its trade deficit ($547.2 billion in 2012), it would boost U.S. GDP by about 4.5 percent ($731 billion) over two years and add six million jobs to the U.S. economy. From these data, it can be deduced that, according to this particular model, reducing trade deficits would have had a 1.33 multiplier on GDP over two years in the U.S. economy, a value higher than any of the multiplier estimates we discussed earlier.

BALANCED TRADE MONETARISM

As we discussed in chapter 6, the fiscally conservative alternative to Keynesianism is called "monetarism." This is the philosophy which holds that monetary policy is extremely effective; therefore the government should maintain more-or-less balanced budgets and let the central bank bring about economic stability by increasing the money supply at a steady rate. This does not mean that the central bank does nothing. The monetarist prescription requires heavy interventions by the central bank during times of recession, when the money supply would normally contract, and requires that the central bank hold down the growth of money supply to prevent much inflation during boom times.

But, as we pointed out in chapter 6, monetary policy has been much less effective since about the 1990s, when the U.S. trade deficits took off. According to research by Martin Feldstein, this is due to the fact that the U.S. capital market has been getting more integrated with the world market.

Integration of the U.S. capital market with the world market has had significant negative consequences for the U.S. trade deficit. One aspect of this integration is the net inflow of foreign savings which accompanies trade deficits and helps drive financial bubbles (chapter 3).

In light of the significant challenges that capital market integration poses for effective monetary policy, controls on the free flow of capital may be warranted. Again we must give John Maynard Keynes credit for preceding us. He was one of the first economists to advocate that capital segmentation was needed for monetary policy to be effective.

For example, on May 23, 1944, in a speech to the House of Lords, he highlighted capital segmentation as one of the primary reasons that he supported the "joint statement" of the allied governments which soon led to the creation of the International Monetary Fund. He pointed out that it upheld the principle that governments can control the inflow and outflow of savings, and thus their own interest rate.

Keynes speech summarized the three monetary principles to which he had devoted the previous thirty years. The first was setting an appropriate exchange rate and the third was preventing deflation. The second was controlling capital movements, specifically:

> We intend to retain control of our domestic rate of interest, so that we can keep it as low as suits our own purposes, without interference from the ebb and flow of international capital movements or flights of hot money. (Keynes 1980b, 16)

Later in the speech, he went into more detail about how the IMF agreement would let Britain control capital flows:

> Let me take first the less prominent of the two issues which arise in this connection, namely, our power to control the domestic rate of interest so as to secure cheap money. Not merely as a feature of transition, but as a permanent arrangement the plan accords to every member government the explicit right to control all capital movements. (Keynes 1980b, 17)

Balancing trade would end the net inflow of savings, effectively segmenting the U.S. economy from the rest of the world. This segmentation could be assisted by high taxes on the interest and dividends earned by foreign savers. At that point, Keynes' stheorizing and Feldstein's studies agree: the Federal Reserve would have more power over unemployment.

The Federal Reserve would also have some new roles regarding the world economy:

1. *Countervailing Currency Interventions.* It should buy and sell foreign currencies to counteract net savings flows into or out of the United States.
2. *Currency Swaps.* In order to maintain international liquidity it should offer sufficient currency swaps to foreign central banks. The growth in dollars abroad should match the need for dollars to finance international transactions.

Meanwhile some of the Federal Reserve's old jobs would continue. It would maintain a growing money supply, sufficient to finance transactions so as to prevent deflation without creating much inflation.

When trade and budgets are relatively balanced, rule-based monetary policy can balance out the business cycle. Milton Friedman recommended that the Federal Reserve keep the money supply growing at a steady 3 percent to 5 percent rate. According to Friedman (Friedman and Friedman 1979, chapter 3), the Great Depression was almost completely caused by a huge contraction of the U.S. money supply and would have cured itself quickly had the Federal Reserve managed to keep the money supply growing.

The combination of balanced trade with balanced budgets suggests a modification to the monetarist policy prescription offered by Friedman and Friedman (chapter 10). Their main rules were: (1) limited spending growth, (2) balanced budgets, and (3) balanced monetary growth. We would add balanced trade to the list.

In this book we have discussed the long-term problems caused by trade deficits, including loss of manufacturing jobs, loss of industries, loss of R&D, and decline in median income. We have also discussed the short-term problems caused by trade deficits, especially high unemployment that has resisted the usual tools of macroeconomic policy. In chapter 9, we proposed a solution to the long-term problems. In this chapter we have proposed a solution to the short term problem, a revision to macroeconomic theory itself. If U.S. policymakers were to balance trade, balance budgets and balance monetary growth, a long period of stable economic growth could ensue.

NOTES

1. Not all economists estimate a multiplier several times greater than one. A study by Valerie A. Ramey and Sarah Zubairy (2013) of the effects of increased U.S. government purchases following unanticipated political and military events from 1898 through 2001, found spending multipliers for government purchases of about 0.8 over the two years following the event and about 0.9 over four years. Studies of recent U.S. economic data have sometimes found even lower multipliers. One of the leading current macroeconomics models is the "New Keynesian" model of the Hoover Institution's John F. Cogan and his coauthors (Cogan et al. 2010). They calculated that an increase in government purchases should be expected to have a multiplier of 0.63 upon GDP when summed over two years. Similarly, Barro and Redlick (2011) found the multiplier to be between 0.6 and 0.7 over two years.

2. The most effective tax cut of all was Reagan's 1986 Tax Reform Act. It greatly reduced marginal tax rates, giving Americans much more incentive to work. According to a study by Nobel Prize winning economist Edward Prescott (2004), Europeans and Americans worked about the same amount of hours in the 1970s when marginal tax rates were about the same on both continents. But by the 1990s, due to the higher marginal tax rates in Europe and the lower ones in the United States, Americans worked many more hours than Europeans. Part of this difference was due to married women entering the labor force in the United States and to Europeans doing more work in non-taxable activities, such as in the underground economy or in home gardens.

References

Aizenman, Joshua, and Jaewoo Lee. 2008. "Financial Versus Monetary Mercantilism: Long-run view of large international reserves holding." *The World Economy*, 31: 593–611.

Alliance for American Manufacturing. 2014. "Findings from a National Survey and Focus Groups of Likely 2014 Voters." Accessed on February 24, 2014. americanmanufacturing .org/files/2014, summary.aam_.National.Poll_.pdf.

Allstate/National Journal. 2010. "Heartland Monitor Poll VII Topline." Accessed on February 10, 2014, allstate.com/resources/Allstate/attachments/heartland-monitor/Heartland_VII_ Topline.pdf.

Ammendola, Giuseppe. 1994. *From Creditor to Debtor: The U.S. Pursuit of Foreign Capital—The Case of the Repeal of the Withholding Tax.* New York: Garland Publishing.

———. 2011. "Some Trends and Perspectives on Globalization, Economic Growth, Equality and Development." *JANUS.NET*, 2 (Autumn): 1–44.

Artus, Patrick. 2012. "What Causes the Dispersion of Savings Rates between Euro-zone Countries?" Flash Economics Economic Research No. 220. Accessed December 22, 2013, cib.natixis.com/flushdoc.aspx?id=63248.

Barbieri, Katherine. 2002. *The Liberal Illusion: Does Trade Promote Peace?* University of Michigan Press.

Barro, Robert J., and Charles J. Redlick. 2011. "Macroeconomic Effects from Government Purchases and Taxes." *The Quarterly Journal of Economics* 126: 51–102.

Bergsten, C. Fred, and Joseph E. Gagnon. 2012. "Currency Manipulation, the US Economy, and the Global Economic Order." Peterson Institute for International Economics, Policy Brief 12–25.

Bernanke, Ben S. 2000. "Japanese Monetary Policy: A Case of Self-Induced Paralysis?" In *Japan's Financial Crisis and its Parallels to U.S. Experience*, edited by Ryoichi Mikitani and Adam S. Posen, 149–166. Washington, DC: Institute for International Economics.

———. 2005. *The Global Saving Glut and the U.S. Current Account Deficit.* Sandbridge Lecture at the Virginia Association of Economics, Richmond, VA, April 14.

———. 2007. *The Level of Economic Well Being.* Remarks at the Greater Omaha Chamber of Commerce, Omaha, NE, February 6.

———. 2009. *Financial Reform to Address Systemic Risk.* Speech at the Council on Foreign Relations, Washington DC, March 10.

———. 2010. *Rebalancing the Global Recovery.* Speech at the Sixth European Central Bank Central Banking Conference, Frankfurt Germany, November 19.

Blecker, Robert A. 2007. "The Economic Consequences of Dollar Appreciation for U.S. Manufacturing Investment: A Time Series Analysis." *International Review of Applied Economics*, 21: 491–517.

Boortz, Neal, and John Linder. 2005. *The Fair Tax Book: Saying Goodbye to the Income Tax and the IRS.* New York: Reagan Books.

Borjas, George J., Richard B. Freeman, Lawrence F. Katz, John DiNardo, and John M. Abowd. 1997. "How Much do Immigration and Trade Affect Labor Market Outcomes?" *Brookings Papers on Economic Activity*, 1997: 1–90.

Brander, James A., and Barbara J. Spencer. 2007. "Export Subsidies and International Market Share Rivalry." *Journal of International Economics* 18: 83–100.

Buchanan, Patrick J. 2011. "How Capital Crushed Labor." September 6. Accessed December 26, 2013, buchanan.org/blog/how-capital-crushed-labor-4861.

Buckley, Chris. 2011. "Global Economic Outlook Grim, China Tells U.S. Trade." *Reuters*, Nov. 21. Accessed December 26, 2013, mobile.reuters.com/article/idUSTRE7AK0BD 20111121?irpc=932.

Buffett, Warren E., and Carol J. Loomis. 2003. "America's Growing Trade Deficit Is Selling the Nation Out from Under Us. Here's a Way to Fix the Problem—and We Need to Do It Now." *Fortune*, November 10.

Bush, George W. 1999. Phoenix Arizona GOP Debate Dec 7, 1999. Accessed on December 28, 2013, www.issues2000.org/Celeb/More_George_W__Bush_China.htm.

Cammarosano, Joseph R. forthcoming. *John Maynard Keynes: Free Trader or Protectionist?* Prepublication manuscript.

Carroll, Mitchell B. 1978. "The Historical Development of Income Tax Treaties." In *Income Tax Treaties*, edited by Jon E. Bischel. New York: Practicing Law Institute.

Cassidy, Robert. 2008. "The Failed Expectations of U.S. Trade Policy: A former U.S. trade negotiator criticizes U.S. trade policy." *Foreign Policy in Focus*, June 4. Accessed December 26, 2013, fpif.org/the_failed_expectations_of_us_trade_policy/.

Chen, Jie. 2013. *A Middle Class Without Democracy: Economic Growth and the Prospects for Democratization in China.* Oxford University Press.

Chen, Jie, and Bruce J. Dickson. 2010. *Allies of the State: China's Private Entrepreneurs and Democratic Change.* Cambridge, MA: Harvard University Press.

Chrinko, Robert S., Steven M. Fazzari, and Andrew P. Meyer. 1999. "How Responsive is Business Capital Formation to its User Cost? An Exploration with Micro Data." *Journal of Public Economics*, 74, 53–80.

Chwieroth, Jeffrey M. 2014. "Managing Capital Inflows: An Exercise in Productive Power." In *Power in a Changing World Economy: Lessons from East Asia*, edited by Benjamin J. Cohen and Eric M.P. Chiu, 69–86. New York: Routledge.

Club for Growth. 2007. "Who Wants to Return to President Hoover's Import Export Trade Policies?" accessed January 2, 2014, www.clubforgrowth.org/projects/?subSec=10.

Cogan, John F., and John B. Taylor. 2012. "What the Government Purchases Multiplier Actually Multiplied in the 2009 Stimulus Package." In *Government Policies and the Delayed Economic Recovery*, edited by Lee Ohanian, John B. Taylor, and Ian Wright, 85–114. Stanford: Hoover Institution Press.

Cogan, John F., Tobias Cwik, John B. Taylor, and Volker Wieland. 2010. "New Keynesian versus Old Keynesian Government Spending Multipliers." *Journal of Economic Dynamics and Control* 34: 281–295.

Corden, W. Max, and J. Peter Neary. 1982. "Booming Sector and De-Industrialisation in a Small Open Economy." *The Economic Journal*, 92: 825–848.

De Bievre, Dirk, and Jappe Eckhardt. 2011. "Interest Groups and the Failure of EU Anti-Dumping Reform." *Journal of European Public Policy*, 8: 338–359.

Der Spiegel. 2010. "Interview with German Finance Minister Schäuble: 'The US Has Lived on Borrowed Money for Too Long.'" *Spiegel Online International*, November 8. www.spiegel.de/international/world/interview-with-german-finance-minister-schaeuble-the-us-has-lived-on-borrowed-money-for-too-long-a-727801.html.

Dickie, Mure. 2008. "Tax Rebates Raised for Chinese Exporters." *Financial Times*, November 12. Accessed December 26, 2013, www.ft.com/intl/cms/s/0/821df3c4-b0db-11dd-8915-0000779fd18c.html.

Dollar, David, and Aart Kraay. 2004. "Trade, Growth, and Poverty." *The Economic Journal* 114: F22–F49.

Dreyfus, Bob. 2010. "China in the Driver's Seat," September 20. Accessed on December 26, 2013, www.thenation.com/article/154484/china-drivers-seat?page=0,0#.

Duncan, Richard. 2005. *The Dollar Crisis: Causes Consequences Cures Revised and Updated.* Singapore: John Wiley and Sons.

Dür, Andreas. 2010. *Protection for Exporters: Power and Discrimination in Transatlantic Trade Relations, 1930–2010.* Cornell University Press.

Espo, David. 2010. "Dems Try to Tap Voter Anger Over Job Loss Overseas." September 18. Accessed on December 26, 2013, www.memphisdailynews.com/editorial/ArticleEmail.aspx?id=52919.

Eurostat. 2014. "Net International Investment Position in % of GDP—Annual Data." Accessed on January 12, 2014, epp.eurostat.ec.europa.eu/tgm/table.do?tab=table&plugin=0&language=en&pcode=tipsii10.

Evans-Pritchard, Ambrose. 2013. "Stocks to Soar as World Money Catches Fire, Calvinist Europe Left Behind." *The Telegraph*, January 1.

Feldstein, Martin. 2005. "Monetary Policy in a Changing International Environment: The Role of Global Capital Flows." NBER Working Paper No. 11856.

Feldstein Martin, and Charles Horoika. 1980. "Domestic Saving and International Capital Flows." *Economic Journal* 90: 314–329.

Fletcher, Ian. 2010. *Free Trade Doesn't Work: What Should Replace It and Why.* Washington, DC: U.S. Business and Industry Council.

Francis, Diane. 2013. "Why Are We Letting China Buy American Companies?" *New York Post*, December 15. Accessed on December 24, 2013, nypost.com/2013/12/15/why-are-we-letting-china-buy-american-companies/.

Friedman, Milton and Rose Friedman. 1979. *Free to Choose: A Personal Statement.* New York: Harcourt Brace Jovanovich.

Gagnon, Joseph E. 2013. *The Elephant Hiding in the Room: Currency Intervention and Trade Imbalances.* Peterson Institute for International Economics Working Paper No. 13–2.

Gehrels, Franz. 1960. "The Unit Terms-of-Trade-Multiplier." *Journal of Economics*, 20: 233–237.

Geithner, Timothy F. 2007. "Developments in the Global Economy and Implications for the United States," January 11. Accessed on December 24, 2013, www.ny.frb.org/newsevents/speeches/2007/gei070111.html.

Goldstein, Morris. 2007. "A (Lack of) Progress Report on China's Exchange Rate Policies, May. Accessed on December 30, 2013, www.iie.com/publications/papers/goldstein0507.pdf.

Gomory, Ralph E. 2010. "A Time for Action: Jobs Prosperity and National Goals." *Huffington Post*, January 25. Accessed on December 26, 2013, www.huffingtonpost.com/ralph-gomory/a-time-for-action-jobs-pr_b_434698.html.

———. 2010b. "The Innovation Delusion." *Huffington Post*, March 1. Accessed on December 26, 2013, www.huffingtonpost.com/ralph-gomory/the-innovation-delusion_b_480794.html.

———. 2010c. "Jobs, Trade and Mercantilism—Part II— Dealing With Reality." *Huffington Post*, September 14. Accessed on December 26, 2013, www.huffingtonpost.com/ralph-gomory/jobs-trade-and-mercantili_b_715954.html.

Gomory, Ralph E., and William J. Baumol. 2000. *Global Trade and Conflicting National Interests*. Cambridge, MA: MIT Press.

Goulder, Lawrence H. 1990. "Implications of Introducing U.S. Withholding Taxes on Foreigners' Interest Income." In *Tax Policy and the Economy*, edited by Lawrence H. Summers. Cambridge, MA: MIT Press.

Gowa, Joanne, and Edward D. Mansfield. 1993. "Power Politics and International Trade." *American Political Science Review* 87: 408–420.

Greenspan, Alan. 2007. *The Age of Turbulence: Adventures in a New World*. New York: Penguin Press.

Harberger, Arnold C. 2006. "Corporation Tax Incidence: Reflections on What Is Known, Unknown and Unknowable." Paper prepared for a Paper prepared for a Conference at the Institute for Public Policy, Rice University, April.

Hart/NewHouse, "NBC/Wall Street Journal GOP Primary Voters Survey." Accessed on December 26, 2013, online.wsj.com/public/resources/documents/WSJ-POLL-20071003.pdf.

Hawkins, John. 2003. "An Interview with Milton Friedman." Accessed on December 26, 2013, www.rightwingnews.com/interviews/an-interview-with-milton-friedman-2/.

Hitselberger, Joseph. 2011. "China Trade Fiasco." Facebook, July 30. Accessed on December 24, 2013, www.facebook.com/groups/327886425672/permalink/10150330603635673/.

Hume, David. (1742). *Part II, Essay V, Of the Balance of Trade*. Indianapolis, IN: Liberty Fund, 1985.

Johnson, David S., Jonathan A. Parker, and Nicholas S. Souleles. 2006. "Household Expenditure and the Income Tax Rebates of 2001." *American Economic Review*, 96: 1589–1610.

Kavilanz, Parija B. 2007. "U.S. Files Piracy Complaint Against China." CNN Money, April 10. Accessed on December 26, 2013, money.cnn.com/2007/04/10/news/international/china_piracy/index.htm.

Keynes, John Maynard. 1936. *The General Theory of Employment Interest and Money*. New York: Harcourt, Brace and Company.

———. 1980a. *The Collected Writings of John Maynard Keynes, Economics Articles and Correspondence: Activities 1940–1944: Shaping the Post-War World*. Volume 25. Edited by Donald Moggridge. London: McMillan, Cambridge University Press.

———. 1980b, *The Collected Writings of John Maynard Keynes, Activities 1941–1946, Shaping the Post-War World Bretton Woods and Reparations*, Volume 26, Edited by Donald Moggridge. London: Macmillan, Cambridge University Press.

———. 1981, *The Collected Writings of John Maynard Keynes, Activities 1929–1931 Rethinking Employment and Unemployment Policies*, Volume 20, Edited by Donald Moggridge. London: Macmillan, Cambridge University Press.

———. 1982, *The Collected Writings of John Maynard Keynes, Activities 1931–1939 World Crisis and Policies in Britain and America,* Volume 21. Edited by Donald Moggridge. London: Macmillan, Cambridge University Press.

Kirk, Ron. 2010. *The President's 2010 Trade Policy Agenda.* Office of the United States Trade Representative. Accessed February 26, 2014, www.ustr.gov/webfm_send/1673.

Kitchen, Michael. 2010. "China to set Anti-Dumping Measures on U.S. Chicken. *Wall Street Journal,* Feb. 5. Accessed on December 26, 2013, www.marketwatch.com/story/china-to-set-anti-dumping-measures-on-us-chicken-2010-02-05.

Krugman, Paul. 1987a. "The Narrow Moving Band, the Dutch Disease, and the Competitive Consequences of Mrs. Thatcher: Notes on Trade in the Presence of Dynamic Scale Economies." *Journal of Development Economics,* 27: 41–55.

———. 1987b. "Is Free Trade Passé?" *Journal of Economic Perspectives,* 1: 131–144.

———. 2010. "Taking on China." *New York Times,* March 14. Accessed on December 24, 2013, www.nytimes.com/2010/03/15/opinion/15krugman.html.

———. 2012. *End This Depression Now!* New York: WW Norton and Company.

Krugman, Paul, and Maurice Obstfeld. 2000. *International Economics: Theory and Policy,* 5th Edition. Glenview, IL: Little, Brown.

Lim, Chong Yah. 2003. "Macroeconomic Management: Is Keynesianism Dead?" *Singapore Economic Review,* 48. DOI: 10.1142/S0217590803000657

Lind, Michael. 2011. "The Cost of Free Trade." *The American Prospect,* December 1. Accessed on December 26, 2013, prospect.org/article/cost-free-trade.

Market Watch. 2010a. "China Says Protectionism Hurting U.S. Trade Ties." *Wall Street Journal,* Feb. 2, 2010. Accessed on December 26, 2013, www.marketwatch.com/story/china-says-protectionism-hurting-us-trade-ties-2010-02-02.

———. 2010b. "China Sets Heavy Anti-Dumping Duty on U.S. Nylon Imports," *Wall Street Journal,* April 22. Accessed on December 29, 2013, from www.marketwatch.com/story/china-sets-97-duty-on-some-us-nylon-imports-2010-04-22?reflink=MW_news_stmp.

McCallum, Bennett. 1999. Theoretical Analysis Regarding a Zero Lower Bound on Nominal Interest Rates. Charnegie Mellon University. Photocopy (September).

Meade, J. E. 1949. "National Income, National Expenditure and the Balance of Payments." *The Economic Journal,* 59: 17–39.

Mellman, Mark, and Whit Ayres. 2010. "AAM 2010 National Survey." Accessed on February 24, 2014, americanmanufacturing.org/files/10pre607-aam-f2-short.pdf.

Meltzer, Allan. 1999. "The Transmission Process." Paper prepared for a conference on the monetary transmission process: recent developments and lessons for Europe, sponsored by Deuche Bundesbank, Frankfurt (25–27 March).

Miller, Terry. 2010. "Obama's Mercantilist Approach to Trade." *The Foundry,* March 3. Accessed on December 26, 2013, blog.heritage.org/2010/03/03/obama%E2%80%99s-mercantilist-approach-to-trade/.

Mitchell, James, Solomos Solumou, and Martin Weale. 2009. "Monthly and Quarterly GDP Estimates for Interwar Britain." *National Institute of Economic and Social Research Discussion Paper,* 348.

Morici, Peter. 2008. "Americans Must Live Beyond their Means." *The Philadelphia Inquirer,* April 6.

Navarro, Peter W., and Greg Autry. 2011. *Death by China: Confronting the Dragon: A Global Call to Action.* Upper Saddle River, NJ: Pearson Prentice Hall.

———. 2012. "Commies in Cadillacs: GM Turns Chinese." *Huffington Post*, May 2. Accessed on December 26, www.huffingtonpost.com/peter-navarro-and-greg-autry/cadillac-china_b_1462711.html.

Obama, Barack H. 2008. "Radio address: President-elect Barack Obama Outlines Economic Recovery Plan." *The Wall Street Journal*, Dec. 6. Accessed on December 24, 2013, online.wsj.com/news/articles/SB122857387293785491.

Obstfeld, Maurice. 1995. *Risk-Taking, Global Diversification, and Growth*. NBER Working Paper No. 4093.

Obstfeld, Maurice, and Kenneth Rogof. 2009. "Global Imbalances and the Financial Crisis: Products of Common Causes." In *Asia and the Global Financial Crisis*, edited by Reuven Glick and Mark M. Spiegel. Federal Reserve Bank of San Francisco.

OECD. 2013. *OECD Economic Outlook*, Vol. 2013(2), OECD Publishing, November. Available on December 26, 2013, dx.doi.org/10.1787/eco_outlook-v2013-2-en.

Ostry, Jonathan D., Atish R. Ghosh, Karl Habermeier, Luc Laeven, Marcos Chamon, Mahvash S. Qureshi, and Annamaria Kokeyne. 2011. "Managing Capital Inflows: What Tools to Use." IMF Staff Discussion Note, SDN/11/06, April 5.

Papadimitriou, Dimitri B., Greg Hannsgen, and Gennaro Zezza. 2008. "The Buffett Plan for Reducing the Trade Deficit." The Levy Economics Institute at Bard College, Working Paper No. 538.

Prasad, Eswar S., Raghuram G. Rajan, and Arvind Subramanian. 2007. "Foreign Capital and Economic Growth," NBER Working Paper No. 13619.

Prescott, Edward C. 2004. "Why do Americans work so much more than Europeans?" NBER Working Paper No. 10316.

President's Advisory Panel on Federal Tax Reform, Final Report. 1998. November 1.

President's Council of Advisors on Science and Technology. 2011. *Report to the President on Ensuring American Leadership in Advanced Manufacturing*. Accessed on December 26, 2013, www.whitehouse.gov/sites/default/files/microsites/ostp/pcast-advanced-manufacturing-june2011.pdf.

Prestowitz, Clyde. 2010. *The Betrayal of American Prosperity: Free Market Delusions, America's Decline, and How We Must Compete in the Post-Dollar Era*. New York: Free Press.

———. 2011. "The Protectionist Humbug." *The FP Group*. Accessed on December 26, 2013, prestowitz.foreignpolicy.com/posts/2011/09/15/the_protectionism_humbug#sthash.vEai3s5m.dpbs.

Ramey, Valerie A. 2011. "Can Government Purchases Stimulate the Economy?" *Journal of Economic Literature*, 49: 673–685.

———. 2012. "Government Spending and Private Activity." In *Fiscal Policy after the Financial Crisis*, edited by Alberto Alesina and Francisco Giavazzi, 19–55. Chicago: University of Chicago Press.

Ramey, Valerie A., and Sarah Zubairy. 2013. *Government Spending Multipliers in Good Times and in Bad: Evidence from U.S. Historical Data*, October 4. Accessed on December 24, 2013, www.econ.ucsd.edu/~vramey/research/RZUS.pdf.

Reinhart, Carmen M., Vincent R. Reinhart, and Kenneth S. Rogoff. 2012. "Public Debt Overhangs: Advanced-Economy Episodes Since 1800." *The Journal of Economic Perspectives*, 26: 69–86.

Reinhart, Carmen M., and Kenneth S. Rogoff. 2013. "Financial and Sovereign Debt Crises: Some Lessons Learned and Those Forgotten." International Monetary Fund Working Paper, December.

Ricardo, David. 1911. *The Principles of Political Economy and Taxation*. London: J. M. Dent and Sons.

Richman, Howard, Raymond Richman, and Jesse Richman. 2009. "Obama Stands By while Europe Loots Intel." *American Thinker*, January 13. Accessed on December 24, www.americanthinker.com/2009/05/obama_stands_by_while_europe_l.html.

———. 2010b. "U.S. Growth Slows Due to Trade Deficit." American Thinker, August 7. Accessed on December 29, 2013, www.americanthinker.com/2010/08/us_growth_slows_due_to_trade_d.html.

Richman, Jesse T., Howard B. Richman, and Raymond L. Richman. 2011. "The Scaled Tariff: A Mechanism for Combating Mercantilism and Producing Balanced Trade." *The Estey Centre Journal of International Law and Trade Policy*, 12: 82–103.

Richman, Raymond L. 2003. "The Great Trade Debate." *Pittsburgh Tribune Review*, September 14.

Richman, Raymond L., Howard B. Richman, and Jesse T. Richman. 2008. *Trading Away Our Future: How to Fix Our Government-Driven Trade Deficits and Faulty Tax System Before It's Too Late*. Pittsburgh: Ideal Taxes Association.

———. 2010a. "The Scaled Tariff would Resuscitate the U.S. Economy." *Enter Stage Right*, July 19. Accessed on January 3, 2014, www.enterstageright.com/archive/articles/0710/0710scaledtariff.htm.

———. 2010c. How to Strengthen the Currency Exchange Rate Reform Bills, House Ways and Means Committee Hearing on China's Exchange Rate Policy, September 15.

Rodrik, Dani. 2013. "In Truth, Mercantilism Never Really Went Away." *The National*, January 11. Accessed on December 26, 2013, www.thenational.ae/business/industry-insights/economics/in-truth-mercantilism-never-really-went-away.

Romer, Christina and Jared Bernstein. 2009. *The Job Impact of the American Recovery and Reinvestment Plan*, January 9.

Sachs, Jeffrey D., Howard J. Shatz, Alan Deardorff, and Robert E. Hall. 1994. "Trade and Jobs in US Manufacturing." *Brookings papers on economic activity* 1994: 1–84.

Samuelson, Paul A. 2004. "Where Ricardo and Mill Rebut and Confirm Arguments of Mainstream Economists Supporting Globalization." *The Journal of Economic Perspectives*, 18: 135–146.

Scissors, Derek. 2011. "Chinese State-Owned Enterprises and U.S.-China Economic Relations." Testimony before the U.S.-China Economic and Security Review Commission, March 30. Accessed on December 26, 2013, www.heritage.org/research/testimony/2011/04/chinese-state-owned-enterprises-and-us-china-economic-relations.

Scott, Robert. 2012. The China Toll: Growing US Trade Deficit with China Cost More than 2.7 Million Jobs between 2001 and 2011. Economic Policy Institute Briefing Paper 345. Downloaded on 12/19/2013 from www.epi.org/publication/bp345-china-growing-trade-deficit-cost/.

Shultz, George P., Michael J. Boskin, John F. Cogan, Allan Meltzer, and John B. Taylor. 2010. "Principles for Economic Revival," *Wall Street Journal*, Sept 16. Accessed on December 26, 2013, online.wsj.com/news/articles/SB10001424052748703466704575489830041633508.

Skidelsky, Robert. 2000. *John Maynard Keynes: Fighting for Freedom 1937–1946*, Volume 3. New York: Viking.

Smith, Adam. 1776. *An Inquiry into the Nature and Causes of the Wealth of Nations*.

Snidal, Duncan. 1985. "Coordination versus Prisoners' Dilemma: Implications for International Cooperation and Regimes." *American Political Science Review*, 79: 923–942.

Sperling, Gene. 2005. *The Pro-Growth Progressive: An Economic Strategy for Shared Prosperity*. New York: Simon and Schuster.

Stamp, J. C. 1931. "The Report of the Macmillan Committee." *The Economic Journal,* 41: 424–435.

Stewart, Terence P., and Elizabeth J. Drake. 2009. "Addressing Balance of Payments Difficulties under World Trade Organization Rules." Economic Policy Institute Working Paper #288.

Taylor, J. B. 2009. "The Lack of an Empirical Rationale for a Revival of Discretionary Fiscal Policy." *The American Economic Review*, 99: 550–550.

Tonelson, Alan. 2010. "Obama Administration's China Trade Brain-Locke." *American Economic Alert*, May 10. Accessed on December 26, 2013, americaneconomicalert.org/view_art.asp?Prod_ID=3498.

Trende, Sean. 2012. "The Case of the Missing White Voters." *Real Clear Politics*, November 8. Accessed on December 27, 2013, www.realclearpolitics.com/articles/2012/11/08/the_case_of_the_missing_white_voters_116106-2.html.

Triffin, Robert. 1960. *Gold and the Dollar Crisis: The Future of Convertibility*. New Haven, CT: Yale University Press.

Trippon, Jim. 2006. "Failure of United States Economic Mission to China Leaves America as Second Fiddle Says China Stock Digest Editor." *China Stock Digest* press release, December 19.

U.S. House of Representatives, 98th Congress, 2nd Session. 1984. *Tax Treatment of Interest Paid to Foreign Persons*, Hearing before the Committee on Ways and Means. Washington, DC: U.S. Government Printing Office, May 1.

Viner, Jacob. 1948. "Power Versus Plenty as Objectives of Foreign Policy in the Seventeenth and Eighteenth Centuries." *World Politics*, 1: 1–29.

Way, Edwin. 2012. "Why Rich Nations Fail: Explaining Dutch Economic Decline in the 18th Century" ExpressO. Accessed on January 1, 2014 at: works.bepress.com/edwin_way/1/.

Weyrich, Paul M., and William S. Lind. 2009. *The Next Conservatism*. South Bend, IN: St Augustine Press.

World Intellectual Property Organization. 2013. "2013 World Intellectual Property Indicators" Accessed on December 13, 2013, www.wipo.int/export/sites/www/freepublications/en/intproperty/941/wipo_pub_941_2013.pdf.

Zou, Heng-fu. 1997. "Dynamic Analysis of the Viner Model of Mercantilism." *Journal of International Money and Finance*, 16: 637–651.

———. 2011. "Foreign Asset Accumulation and Macroeconomic Policies in a Model of Mercantilism," China Economics and Management Academy Working Paper No. 432.

Index

About the Authors

Jesse Richman is associate professor of political science at Old Dominion University, and received his PhD from the political economy program at Carnegie Mellon University. His work has appeared in a range of academic journals including the *American Political Science Review*, the *Review of Law and Economics, Legislative Studies Quarterly, State Politics and Policy Quarterly*, and the *Estey Centre Journal of International Law and Trade Policy*. He teaches courses in game theory, quantitative methods, and American politics.

Howard Richman holds a PhD from the University of Pittsburgh. He co-authored numerous articles in theoretical psychology when he worked with Economics Nobel Laureate Herb Simon at Carnegie Mellon University, and now teaches economics on the Internet. He is research associate at the Ideal Taxes Association.

Raymond Richman is professor emeritus of public and international affairs at the University of Pittsburgh. He received his doctorate in economics from the University of Chicago under the direction of Milton Friedman. He served briefly as head of the Departments of Economics at the University of Illinois at Chicago and the University of Massachusetts at Amherst. He served for many years as a consultant to the World Bank, the IMF, the Inter-American Development Bank, and the U.S. Agency for International Development, participating in and heading missions to Panama, Colombia, Central America, and Egypt. He also served as a consultant to the Asian Development Bank.

CPSIA information can be obtained at www.ICGtesting.com
Printed in the USA
BVOW05*0618160414

350755BV00002B/2/P

9 780739 188804